i love Him,
i love Him not,
i finally love Him

discovering a real love for God

i love Him,
i love Him not,
i finally love Him

discovering a real love for God

Laurie Russell

Russell Media

Boise, Idaho

Published in Boise, Idaho by Russell Media
Web: http://www.russell-media.com

Cover and text Design by Woohoo Ink, LLC

This book may be purchased in bulk for educational, business, organizational, or promotional use.

For information please email info@russell-media.com.

ISBN (print): 978-1-937498-15-3
ISBN (ebook): 978-1-937498-16-0

Printed in the United States of America

note to the reader

Some of the names and details have been changed in order to protect the guilty, ahem, I mean innocent.

To Noah and Anastasia,
you are my jewels,
a treasure given to me by God.

acknowledgments

I have longed to write a book ever since I was a child. But like my other childhood dreams for the future, (like becoming a professional soccer player or winning an Olympic Gold Medal in the Marathon), I pushed that desire to the side. That all changed when I saw that God had assembled around me family and friends who wanted me to achieve this dream. To these and others, I offer my sincere gratitude. But I especially want to thank:

My husband, *Mark,* the man of my dreams and best friend. You are my number one cheerleader. You gave me courage to share my story and never let me give up when I felt defeated. I love you, Mark, and I couldn't have completed this work without you! Forever is wonderful with you in my life.

My kiddos, *Noah and Anastasia.* You are my heart. There was a part of me that was empty until Jesus put you in my life. I now have a glimpse of the love God feels toward His children. Thank you, my jewels, for allowing me to share some of our stories in this book. I promise never to serve you dinner off the floor again and if I do, I pledge to at least sweep up the dog hair first.

My parents, *Mark and Carol*, my first exposure to unconditional love. Thank you, Mom and Dad, for standing by me through all my crazy adventures. Your support has been the rock that held me steady and the base I needed to step out in faith. Thank you for your continued encouragement, especially as I wrote.

My siblings, *Beth and Brian*. You prayed me through my rebellious years and I am a better person because of you two. Thank you for the numerous times you read the various drafts of this book over the years. The hours you gave are priceless. God used our long walks and talks to mold me into the person I am today. I am blessed to have siblings I love with all my heart!

My extended family, *Russells, Deatons, Muchers and Wilsons*. Thank you for the many ways you love and support us. Thank you for watching the kids so I could get in extra writing and for being a sounding board as I processed my work. I love you all!

My editors, *Anna McHargue*, thank you for the many hours you spent reading and rereading this work and for sitting with me at my desk working tirelessly until the book found its rhythm. You have talent, girlfriend! God knew I needed an editor as a friend. Thank you for never turning me away! *Andrea Kellner*, thank you for your patience in working with this grammatically challenged writer. You are a beautiful wordsmith and that has only made my writing better. *Rebecca Ross*, my niece. You are beautiful both inside and out. Thank you for sharing your editing skills. You're a gifted writer and it shows through your edits and suggestions. I look forward to reading your next book! *Colleen Maile*, thank you for sharing your proofing skills. Your insight was so helpful and put the finishing touches on the book.

To *Andy Fraser* and *Woohoo*, thank you for you for all your help in developing this book from cover design to layout. Thank you for your belief in me and for the many hours you gave promoting it. You are a blessing.

To *Leslie Hertling*, thank you for help with layout design. You have a great eye and did a great deal to enhance the book. So glad we found you!

Ryan Hanson and *Bobby Kuber*, thanks for the many roles you play at Russell Media. Your comic relief is always a great stress reliever. We could not make it without you guys!

And most importantly, my *Lord and Savior, Jesus.* Thank you for not giving up on me. Thank you for hearing my plea and cry for help. The journey was rough and long at times but You never left me alone. I can't imagine life without You. I love You, I truly love You!

contents

introduction

God loves you.

Growing up in church, this was always something I assumed. I heard numerous stories in Sunday school of how He loved me and how His original plan was for all of us to spend eternity with Him in heaven. Heaven sounded great, especially when I considered the alternative. (Hell was hot and heat makes me crabby and my hair nappy and I didn't want to spend eternity with frown lines and frizzy hair.) In church I was taught the basic tenet of the Christian faith: our sin separates us from God but Jesus provided a way for us to get back to God when He died on the cross, thus paying the price for our sins.

Jesus had given us a huge gift and my job was to love Him and I did, kind of, but I was told to love my younger sister, too, and anyone who has siblings knows that it's not always easy to love someone you're "supposed to" love — at least when you are a kid. So I assumed the same would hold true for God. In a sense He was my personal superhero — the only one left that really existed. I had lost Santa Claus, the Easter Bunny, and all the other "special people" in the life of a child. It felt comforting to know that one still remained.

As I grew, I was confronted with all sorts of worldly distractions. Friends, television, books, magazines, and even strangers began to influence what I believed and who I wanted to become. I stepped away from God during my college years, mainly because I believed following Jesus put a damper on all my fun. I was a really good sinner; a gold medal winner, if there were such an event.

One night, I went out dancing with some friends. It was a horrible night and we left feeling empty and depressed. On the car ride home my friend Abby said, "There has to be more to life than this!" I agreed. The next weekend she visited a big church in our area. The following Sunday she took me with her. Overnight we went from hanging out in bars to scoping out the singles scene at church. We weren't necessarily seeking spiritual guidance as much as we were nice-looking Christian men. But, hey, we were young and God knew how to lure us back into the church.

We didn't find the men but in time we did find God. Four months after I began attending I heard a sermon on faith and something clicked. It wasn't a spiritual statement that I could regurgitate but an understanding of who God was in my life. I didn't know all the facts about God but something in my heart changed and I immediately knew I couldn't go back to my old life. I felt as if I finally had been released from my burden of guilt and now felt energetic and free.

After this, I wanted to talk about God nonstop. I attended Bible studies and prayer groups, although I was always too nervous to pray out loud. I read books about God. I couldn't get enough. I was infatuated with Him. People around me talked in a different language, saying things like, "I've been backsliding and wrestling with my old self so I had a long quiet-time." Or, "God told me to fast for three days. By God's grace I now am free." At first I thought they had done something inappropriate while mudwrestling and were put into a spiritual version of time out. But after a while I understood the gist of what they were saying and before long, I was using similar terminology (even though I never fully comprehended what I was saying).

Once I learned to talk the talk, I began to walk the walk and I got busy. I volunteered in the nursery (even though I didn't know how to change a diaper). I worked in the soup kitchen (even though I didn't know how to cook). I went on mission trips (even though I didn't know much about the Bible). I wanted to give back to God because He had "set me free" (Christianese definition: removed the burden and guilt that my sins had placed on me). But after a while I began to feel guilty if I said "no" to requests for my time and was soon resentful of all my service.

I was now carrying a new set of burdens: the burden of "I ought to" or "If I were a *good* Christian then I would" and on and on. Where did these come from? No one had given them to me.

I once read a quote that said, "You can serve someone without loving them, but you can't love someone without serving them." What did it mean about my love for God if I couldn't serve Him with a joyful heart? Did I not have *real* love for God?

Perhaps in my eagerness to be a committed follower of God, I rushed through a valuable phase required in developing a true love for God. When my husband Mark and I began dating, we went through an infatuation phase. I personally think infatuation is a good thing for all relationships and serves a purpose. It provided adrenaline that enabled us to talk late into the night on the phone, and spend endless hours in coffee shops gathering more information and learning about each other. This investment of time allowed us to then determine whether or not to take our relationship to the next level of commitment.

However, a relationship can't stay in the infatuation phase long; our bodies and minds can't hold up to the lack of sleep and we eventually have to pop out of our daydreaming about our significant other and rejoin the rest of the world. Real life sets in, infatuation fades, and the couple learns to engage in life together, and, if they are committed, they work to keep the love relationship alive.

Before Mark and I married, we went through premarital counseling. One thing our counselor, Bob, noticed is that we both avoided conflict. Mark would retreat while I, on the other hand, would hold anger in for a long while and then explode in resentment leaving Mark to wonder if he needed to have me exorcised. Bob coached us on how to pick topics that needed to be addressed and then how to share and actively listen to one another.

Over the years this has helped our love and companionship grow by removing obstacles that otherwise would stunt their growth. We're far from perfect and there are still times that I emotionally erupt and Mark goes into hiding, but we're now able to see the outburst as a red flag and a reminder that we need to reopen our lines of communication and seek out what is *hindering* our love from growing even deeper.

I had fully embraced the infatuation phase with God but once the giddiness of my new life with God began to fade, I tried to replace it with the "feel good" adrenaline of serving, whether or not I felt called by God to do it. Every "thank you" and accolade fueled me to the next project. I had spent so much of my time being the "bad girl" that it felt nice to be the good girl finally and it was addictive.

Our spiritual life is often described as a series of mountaintop experiences where God reveals bits of heaven. These glimpses energize and strengthen us for the time when we inevitably will face difficult challenges in the valley. But our time in the valley is where we engage heart-to-heart with God, actively communicating and listening. We fervently seek Him. We ask "why?" and "how long?" begging Him to show Himself to us. This is where God can reveal hindrances that block us from truly developing a love for Him. However, if we're too busy trying to find the next feel-good moment, we miss this opportunity to truly get to know God. When we truly know God, we can't help but truly love Him.

Because I had not spent time in the valley with God, over the years my burdens had become heavy. There were some things about God that bugged me, made me nervous and at times really mad. In the past, whenever these feelings arose, I'd excuse them away, claim "faith" and then get busy serving in the hopes of quickly climbing my way out of the present valley.

Why did I do this? Perhaps part of me feared learning something about God that I didn't want to know. Maybe God really was an arrogant bully. Maybe Jesus spoke in a monotone and only performed miracles to show off and keep the crowds interested. Maybe I would learn that God was absentminded? I mean, how can a loving God allow someone with a weapon to enter an elementary school and shoot innocent children and adults? I wondered if He either was not paying attention or simply didn't care. Why didn't He stop the tsunami? Why did He let my grandfather, who I really, *really* loved, die so young?

My questions and doubts were nothing new but they were hindering me from developing a true love relationship with God. Instead of a growing love for God, I was beginning to feel burned out, resentful, and even bitter. I wasn't excited about going to church on Sunday morning and was envious of my neighbor, who was still in his bathrobe, sipping a cup of coffee while reading the morning newspaper. My questions and doubts not only hindered my love for God but also my ability to fully see His love for me.

I had a choice. I could stuff these doubts and hope that things would get better in time, or I could ask God and see if He would give me some direction. One thing was for certain: I couldn't fake it much longer. God was either worth my love or a waste of my time.

I knew life wouldn't be perfect here on Earth and I've never been accused of being a genius but I knew enough that an abundant life didn't equal a depleted life. I also knew that true love for another can give you the extra edge to go the extra mile and I needed that with God. I wanted to have that love for God. I just didn't know how to get it.

chapter 1

i don't love God

Why do I always procrastinate?

I sat down at our dining room table and opened the Bible study I was doing with a group of fellow missionaries. I had been putting off my weekly homework until the last minute each week, like I did writing term papers in college. There was a time when I enjoyed the daily lessons and focused time with God, but lately it felt more like an obligation.

For some reason, today was even worse. I had struggled through the first lesson and on the second and third ones I had trouble concentrating and was feeling a little agitated. By day four's lesson, a sourness lurked within me and I was tempted to pull out a black marker, color the page and mail it back to the publisher. Maybe I was hormonal — I did have a three-month-old — but this didn't feel like a physiological issue. It was more internal; a heaviness in my soul that drained me — a spiritual burnout.

The author talked often of her love for God and kept saying, "I just *love* the Lord!" Her words grated on me, and the more I read them, the more they irked me. It wasn't her personally — even though I could hear her voice as I read each word. I liked her and had enjoyed her other studies. It was *what* she was saying. It reminded me of the days I was single and one of my friends would talk endlessly of her love for her fiancé. Sure I was happy for my friend but deep down there was a part of me that ached to love another that way also.

I was tempted to skip the rest of the homework and play the new mother card: "He's been so colicky lately that I haven't been able to feed the rest of us, much less do my homework." But I figured it was only a matter of time until this really did happen (and maybe it counts as a double sin to lie at a Bible study?) so I decided to stick it out.

Perhaps a cup of tea would help. As I waited for the water to boil, I wondered why I was bothered hearing her talk about loving God. She loved God and that's a good thing. I love Him, too, right? I felt kind of numb. I tried to remember the last time I told someone I loved God? Hmm . . . when was the last time I said it to myself?

I couldn't think of it.

"Do I love God? Do I really love Him?"

I never had asked myself this question before and I suddenly realized that I didn't have the answer. I wanted to say yes but I didn't honestly know. How can I be sure that I truly love God? I can't look into His eyes and see His love for me. How do I know that He's really watching over me? How can I feel His love for me when I can't embrace Him? How do I know for sure? The ache in my stomach returned but this time it wasn't directed toward the Bible study's author, it was directed toward myself. "Do I love God? Do I really love Him?" My heart wouldn't allow the words to form. I couldn't say it.

"Oh, my gosh, I don't think I love Him. I don't. I don't love God!"

I sat there, stunned, having just discovered a hidden truth. My faith and everything I had known to be true and based my life upon, like a house of cards came crashing down. I looked at my son Noah, who slept next to me in his bouncy seat. I loved him with all my being. I could sit and talk with people about him all day long. I loved serving and caring for him. I never wanted to be away from him. I would give my life to keep him safe. Why did I not feel a love this deep for God?

I wanted to but I didn't and it was nauseating to hear this ring in my head.

Noah must have sensed my thoughts and he began to cry for his next feeding. The duties of the day trumped my Bible study and took away the time to give serious thought to this question. Maybe it would all go away. I'm the queen of being able to push aside painful thoughts; plus, it wasn't a comfortable question to ponder. I had grown up in the church and was now serving in full-time ministry, as a missionary living overseas, of all things. It was impossible that I didn't really love God.

Maybe it *was* hormones and lack of sleep.

❖ ❖ ❖

Louisa greeted me at the door. She was hosting our Bible study that consisted of eight women with ages varying from twenty-one to sixty-five. Noah was asleep in his carrier so I placed him on the floor and sat down next to him as we began going over the homework. I had done well at hiding my episode from earlier that day but it had left me with a heavy heart full of apathy. As we went through each day's homework this feeling grew.

When we reached day four my heart pounded nervously the way it does before public speaking — I actually felt winded even though I was just sitting on the floor. What was going on? An urge to share my concerns from earlier moved in me but then a huge lump vacillated between my stomach and throat and I feared my body was about to do something embarrassing.

Others in the group were talking so I had an excuse not to say anything. No need to be rude and talk over someone. Hopefully they would keep talking and move to the next point before the lump exploded, but then the room became quiet. There was a long, almost awkward, pause that seldom happened in this group of talkative women.

Should I share? Perhaps they are feeling the same way, too, or have experienced this before and could help me process my feelings. These are my friends.

But what would they think of me? I was a missionary and missionaries don't go around telling people they have lost their love for God. What if one of them reported this to our supervisors, even if out of concern for me? Would Mark and I lose our jobs? Would we be sent home? Where does a "fired" missionary find work? How would we support our growing family? I wasn't sure what I would face. Would it be compassion or judgment?

I began talking, but about something totally unrelated. I was not quite sure what I was saying. I'm sure I sounded like Charlie Brown's teacher, "Wah wah, wah wah, wah wah." Everyone looked on at me with encouraging smiles and nods. As I spoke, I thought to myself, "I really like these women. They are safe. I can trust them with my doubts." Without warning, the words burst out of my mouth, like the spontaneous eruption of a volcanic geyser, "I don't think I love God anymore."

[Insert record scratch]

Oh, no, big mistake! Take it back, take it back!

If only I could. I hadn't given my delivery of this news much forethought and it showed. The smiles faded. One of them looked as if I had punched her in the stomach. Another tried to continue smiling but the lack of oxygen she was experiencing put more of a twisted smile on her lips and fear in her eyes. The other faces displayed a mixture of emotions and some looked down to avoid making eye contact with me.

There was another awkward silence and I was afraid to say anything else for fear of making it worse. Finally, one of the older women in the group spoke up, "Of course you love God. You're just in the middle of a major life change. You have a new baby and live in a foreign country. That's a lot of new things to deal with. You'll feel better soon."

Nods spread around the room. Her advice had some truth to it. There *were* new stressors in my life and I could probably convince myself to blame my outburst on them, but something told me that wasn't it. It felt more as if these stressors had only revealed to me a deeper internal issue. Either way, it appeared that God was trying to tell me something and based on my history with God, He wasn't going to allow the problem to go away easily.

My face contorted as I fought back tears. Why do I always open my mouth and say stupid stuff at Bible study? (Note to self: at Bible study it is safer to share embarrassing body noises than your true feelings.) The awkward silence returned and one of the other ladies changed the subject and the topic was dropped and not addressed again. But, a few pairs of eyes met my gaze, almost as if they understood what I was trying to say.

We continued with the study and I did my best to pretend everything was normal and everyone else did the same. But I wondered, "What is normal? What is it like to really love God? Have I ever truly loved Him or have I yet to fully develop love? Was it even possible to have a 'real' love for an invisible God here on Earth?" I was grateful for all He had done for me but does deep gratitude equate with love?

At the end of the study we ate snacks and chatted about weekend plans. Afterwards I grabbed Noah and we headed out to the car. I placed his carrier into his car seat and kissed his tiny head. My love for him grew and developed daily. If only I could have this with God.

❈ ❈ ❈

Mark and I sat at the table eating dinner that night. We had recently celebrated our second wedding anniversary. We had met seven years prior when we both were preparing to go to Russia as missionaries. We were platonic friends for the first four years, but then, one summer, something changed in both of us and we were married the following June.

Our four years of friendship provided a strong base in our relationship. On the mission field, Mark had seen me at my worse and at my best. Over the years I talked openly to him about my belief system, never feeling the need to put up a front to impress him because we were, after all, just friends.

Our relationship was solid, so why was I afraid to share my new doubts with him? Would he be angry that I disclosed it at my Bible study before sharing it with him? What if we were sent home as the shamed missionaries who were fired because the wife "lost her faith?" Would he regret marrying me? Surely he wouldn't leave me and choose his ministry over his family! I guess I felt it best to wait this out and share it later. Maybe it all would just go away.

Mark had work to do on the computer that night so I told him that I'd clean up. I collected the dishes and walked into the kitchen when Mark asked me, "How was Bible study today?"

Not knowing how to answer I replied, "Good." My heart rate increased and the lump in my throat reappeared. Even though I was scared, part of me wanted to share this with Mark, knowing he'd be the one person to help me process it. I peered from the kitchen into the office. He was already on the computer and I knew he'd only be half-listening, so, I threw him some bait.

"I think I made a fool of myself today."

He chuckled, "Oh yeah, how's that?"

"I told the group that I don't think I love God anymore."

[Insert record scratch again]

Mark slowly walked into the kitchen, "Why did you say that?"

It was a genuine question but I was at the breaking point and the next thing I knew, the lump that had been in my throat the whole day finally emerged and exited in a flood of anger. I was getting tired of others doubting my doubts.

"Because I don't, Mark! I don't want to talk about Him. I am bored when I read the Bible. I have absolutely no desire to talk to others about Him. Serving Him used to be an honor but now it feels like an obligation. And, if He were in this room right now and asked me if I loved Him, I honestly couldn't tell Him that I do. I *don't* love God. I don't *love* Him. I no longer feel love toward God!" Strangely, my verbal explosion felt good.

Mark was stunned and stood there staring at me. I think he was waiting for my head to spin 360 degrees while I projectile vomited. He walked over to me and wrapped his arms around me. My anger melted into sobs. He then said, "I think we should pray about this. Be honest with God about the way you are feeling and we'll trust Him to help us work this out."

My initial desire was to punch him in the stomach. Had I not just told him that I have no desire to pray?! I quickly reminded him of it and he said, "Okay, I'll pray then and you can afterwards, if you'd like."

When I was a kid, I stole a piece of bubblegum from the local corner store. Afterwards, each time I saw a cop, I thought he was looking for me. My mom caught me chewing the gum so I decided to confess my larceny to my parents. I knew it would hurt and disappoint them and that a punishment would follow. As Mark prayed, I wondered if the same would happen with God? He already knew the condition of my heart but how would He respond to me acknowledging it? Would He punish me or remove His blessings? Would God see me as unworthy?

Would *He* still love me?

I didn't know but I couldn't keep living a lie.

Mark finished praying and I sat there for a second,

not knowing what to say. Mark kept hugging me and said, "Just tell God what you feel. Be honest."

I didn't want to talk with God but I figured it was the least I could do. "God, I've lost my love for you and I don't know what to do. I read the Bible and it does nothing for me. I try to pray to You but my mind wanders and I can't connect with You. I'm tired of talking about You and have lost my desire to share You with others. I'm having doubts. I want to love You but I don't know how. Please . . . help me. Help me know how to truly love You."

For the first time that day I felt a break in the heaviness within me. I didn't feel "fixed" but my burden seemed lighter. An ounce of hope had returned to me. God had shown me the root cause of my burnout. I had lost my passion and desire to pursue Him and develop a deeper love for Him. Maybe God would come through and help me rekindle this love.

chapter 2

does God love me?

What do you do when you don't love God?

The days following my Bible study outburst, I felt happier and more like my old self. I knew the source of my "burnout on God." It finally had been identified so all I had to do was fix the problem. But how do you develop a love relationship with an invisible God, especially when you thought you loved Him already? I was not aware of a support group for people who no longer love God. What was my next step? John the Baptist and the disciples had the benefit of seeing Jesus in the flesh. They could look into His eyes and see His sincerity. They could feel His embrace and know it was heartfelt. They could hear His voice and sense that His words were authentic.

It's easier to fall in love with someone when you know they love you back. The disciples had God in the flesh; they knew His love was real. How could I be sure that God loved me? "Does God love *me*?" I was wavering in my love for Him but did He struggle to love me, too? I'll be the first to tell you that I'm not an easy one to love, and with so many of us on the planet, it seemed like it would be easy for Him to choose me not to love personally.

Perhaps this was a good place for me to start. I needed to know. It didn't seem possible to fully love God if I didn't know for sure that He loved me back. So I prayed, "God, is your love for me generic or do you truly love *me*?" I didn't hear anything or feel anything but I made a commitment to keep asking God until I heard from Him. I'd be like the nagging widow that Jesus talked about in Luke 18 when He taught His disciples not to give up on prayer.

Three events in life bonded my mother and me: planning my wedding and the births of our two kids, Noah and Anastasia. Noah, our first child, was born in Santiago, Chile. Unfortunately, my mom has a severe fear of flying and was unable to come visit us to meet Noah. It was an emotional time for me to go through his birth without her nearby. We were not scheduled to travel back to the States until nine months later. Long distance calling was pricier back then and it was expensive for me to call her and talk about Noah or ask her questions about being a mother. When we did speak, the calls always ended with lots of tears. I always had dreamed of sharing this time in my life with my mother. I wanted to watch her be a grandmother with my kids the way I had seen her with my nieces and nephews. I felt so alone as a new mother in a foreign country.

One morning, about a month after the Bible study episode, as I dressed for the day, my heart ached for my mother and I cried out again to God, "Please can I see her and let her meet Noah?" It felt foolish to pray this; I knew there was no way for it to happen. But this time, instead of silence, I heard a voice in my head saying, "Go home and see her." It was my own inner voice but it was different this time, more authoritative. Surely it was my mind playing tricks on me. However, I had a strong peace in my heart that moved me to action.

I ran downstairs and told Mark that God had just told me to go home and take Noah to see my mom. I could tell immediately he had not heard the same voice and was concerned it was most likely postpartum hormones speaking, not God. (Hormones get the blame for a lot of things in our household.) "Uh, are you sure? We don't have the money to fly you home and we'll have to get permission for you to leave work and go back to the States." He was being a killjoy so I told him that time would tell if it was God or not. In the meantime, I was going to look for Internet deals for flights back home.

I scoured the Internet for cheap flights. Each day I'd search different websites looking for "the deal" that I knew God was going to send to my inbox, but each day was met with disappointment. I began to doubt and wonder if my own desire to go home had tricked me into thinking I had heard God telling me to look for tickets. I was embarrassed that I had voiced it to Mark and felt foolish for believing it myself.

One day after I did my morning routine of checking for flights, I looked over and saw Mark standing in the doorway watching me. There was pain in my eyes. My voice betrayed me when I told him the prices were still too high. "I was so sure it was God telling me to go home. Why would He tease me with hope only to let me down?" We didn't know how to make this trip home happen but my emotions must have moved Mark into action. He began researching ways to get me home when a new idea hit him. His brother, Jeff, worked for a consulting firm and traveled a great deal. He and his colleagues earned numerous frequent flyer miles, so Mark emailed and asked him if he knew of anyone who would be willing to sell some miles to us for a cheaper price.

A couple of days later I was cooking dinner when Mark ran in and said, "It looks like you're going home, baby! God just sent you a ticket!"

"What?! Really? How?"

Jeff and his soon-to-be wife, Tara, ran a nonprofit organization on the side that utilized business professionals and their skills to help developing countries around the world. The previous year he had led a volunteer team to work with us in Santiago. One of Jeff's colleagues was on that team and had seen Jeff's email and then forwarded it to his father who also traveled for work. The father wrote Jeff and told him of the positive impact the mission trip had on his son. He was grateful to Jeff and our team for hosting him and offered me all the miles I needed for a round-trip ticket . . . free of charge! Not only were Noah and I going to see my family, but it wasn't going to cost us anything.

A few weeks later we received all the paperwork needed for Noah and me to leave the country. Our mission agency was very supportive and gave approval for me to go home for a week and, within days, Noah and I were boarded and on our way to Virginia. Our final flight landed in Greensboro, North Carolina. It was a puddle jumper plane that had us disembark on the runway. These were the pre 9/11 days when family or friends could meet you at your arriving gate. As I walked toward I gate, I looked up and saw my parents watching us from the window. They waved excitedly. I couldn't believe my prayers had been answered. My parents rushed to us as we walked through the door. My father snapped a beautiful shot of my mother and Noah seeing each other for the first time. It was perfect.

Our trip was short but it was exactly what my mother and I needed. We did all the typical mother-daughter-grandchild things. We shopped for baby clothes; she gave me tips on how to transition Noah to cereal; we took tons of pictures and drank tea and talked. It was a week full of memories made as a mother passed down wisdom to her daughter.

On the way back to Chile, we had to fly through Miami. Our plane pulled away from the gate, taxied a bit, and then stopped. Mechanical problems were the cause but we remained on the airplane for three hours. It was stuffy and I was nervous as Noah wiggled restlessly in my arms. This trip had been my first time to fly with an infant and I was learning the ropes by myself. The two gentlemen next to me were Chilean and they spoke perfect English. One of them asked if he could hold Noah to give me a break and they were soon taking turns playing with him as I filled out our declaration forms needed for customs.

Around 11:00 p.m., the pilot announced they were canceling our flight and that we were returning to the gate and would be overnighting in Miami. The airline put us all in a nice hotel along with plenty of food vouchers. My two Chilean seatmates had, by this time, adopted me as their granddaughter and spoke to the airline employees, insisting that Noah and I get to the hotel soon. We were escorted to a shuttle and quickly off to our hotel.

The next morning I ran into them at breakfast. They informed me that other flights to Santiago were already booked and that we needed to get to the airport soon. They met me in the lobby, carried my luggage, and told me they would help get Noah and me home. At the airport, they argued in Spanish with the LanChile airline employees to find a seat for me on the next flight, telling them Noah and I had already had a long journey and needed to be reunited with Mark. Within an hour they handed me a boarding pass, we said our goodbyes, and I never saw them again. They were like angels, aiding me in a stressful time.

It was a long trip home but in a weird way, it had been a fulfilling adventure. Mark was waiting for us outside of the international terminal. It had been a hard separation for him and he immediately scooped Noah from my arms while kissing me — it was a wonderful reunion. At home I shared with him all the fun we had with my parents and then how overwhelmed I was changing Noah's diaper on an airplane for the first time or figuring out how to get a stroller and my carry-on into a bathroom stall at the same time and the fiasco with our flight cancelation. I relayed the many ways my seatmates helped us, "I don't know if I would have made it onto my flight without them. It was as if God placed us together, knowing they would help me."

Mark leaned over and kissed me, "You can't deny that God loves you."

Nope, I couldn't. This trip was a gift, a *personal* gift from God. Prior to telling Mark of my yearning to visit my mom, I had not communicated to anyone my desire to see my mom but had only shared it in my prayer time with God. I now knew He had heard my prayer and understood the desire of my heart. He spoke to me personally and I believe that it was He who not only told me to go home but then also provided the passage for me to get home at no cost. He then worked a miracle in my favor, using the compassion and generosity of family, friends, and even strangers in order to fulfill the desire of my heart. He had done all of this for me. I felt like a daughter whose father had seen her hurting and did everything in his power to bring her joy and to comfort her.

No longer could I say that my lack of love for God came because He neglected to love me. He had lavished me with His love.

How great is the love the Father has lavished on us,
that we should be called children of God!
And that is what we are.
1 John 3:1

is love an obligation?

What are my expectations of God?

God had made it clear that He loved me. I needed that. It's wonderful being loved, but to be honest, just because someone loves you doesn't necessarily mean you love him or her back. It sounds harsh but it's true. At various times I have been on either side of that scenario: hopelessly in love with another who didn't reciprocate my feelings or vice versa. We all know that neither option feels good.

One friend told me he thought that it wasn't possible for us to truly love God until we are in heaven, see Him face to face and see all that He is and all that we aren't. In some part that may be true. I'm sure our love for Him will go to a whole new level at that moment, but when questioned, Jesus said the greatest commandment is for us to love God with all of our heart, soul, and mind (Matthew 22:37). Was He saying that if we master this first, the desires of our hearts will naturally align with God's and then following and obeying Him will come more easily or more naturally?

Initially I worried what my failing love for God meant about my faith. Did it make me a non-believer? Was I no longer considered a child of God? I didn't think so. I still believed in God and the Bible, and still considered Jesus my Savior. The fact that I was addressing the issue and not blowing it off showed me that I was committed to God. The problem instead was that I had fallen out of love with God. Since God is perfect and I am a sinner, the odds suggested that my lack of love had to do with me, not Him.

I was searching for any way that would help me develop my love for God. Was He a bully? Was He boring or weird? Was I inappropriately applying human characteristics to God to figure out if this is why I didn't love Him anymore? I began looking at the forms of love I felt as a child, a parent, and a wife in hopes of understanding what I look for in love and what has caused me to lose love for another. I then made a list of the characteristics and qualities of these people and considered if I found them in God. Was I wrong to look for human qualities in my love for God? We are made in His image but was I selfishly trying to make Him into the "God of *my* dreams?"

The Bible is filled with stories of the Israelites and their neighbors creating images of gods to fill their personal needs. Even today, I'm sure I'm guilty of interpreting and manipulating our understanding of God in order to make Him into the one *I* want Him to be. But I wanted to have a real love for the *real* God and in order for that to happen, I would have to work harder in getting to know Him and asking Him some hard questions.

❋ ❋ ❋

The following months I continued to think more about it and realized that these emotions and qualities I longed to find in God were hindrances that were preventing me from truly *loving* God. Whether or not they were legit, I wasn't sure, but I had to trust the words I'd read in Hebrews 11:6, "We must believe that God is real and that he rewards everyone who searches for him" (CEV). However, if I was searching out love for God, it would require that I address the hard questions. But part of me wondered, "Is it okay to question God? Is it disrespectful?"

I wasn't sure. I mean He is the Creator of all things. He is the one who turned Lot's wife into a pillar of salt because she disobeyed Him. I didn't want to end up a future salt lick for some horse because I dishonored God, but at the same time, I knew I needed to address these questions. So I flipped through the Gospels in search of others who cornered God with hard questions and to see if it would give me some direction.

As I read various stories it appeared Jesus' response was dependent upon the heart of the one inquiring. With the Pharisees and Sadducees He was pretty harsh — not that I blame Him. They were constantly trying to expose Him as a fake and deter others from following Him — that would get old after a while. But when He was approached by a teacher of the law and questioned about the greatest commandment, He responded more gently and ended their dialogue with, "You are not far from God's kingdom" (Mark 12:34 CEV). Did He see something different in this man? Was he someone truly seeking the truth?

However, these men were not followers of Jesus and I needed to see how He responded when one of His own doubted. The first to pop into my mind was John the Baptist, the hairy one who paved the way for Jesus. He was Jesus' cousin. He was family. He baptized Jesus and announced Him as the awaited Messiah. He even heard God's voice boom out of heaven after he baptized Jesus, "You are my Son, whom I love; with him I am well pleased." If there were anyone who shouldn't have doubt, you'd think it would have been John.

Then again, John had a good reason to doubt. He had devoted the majority of his adult life to preparing the way of Jesus' ministry. He had given up luxuries and sacrificed much to serve God. But despite his devotion and sacrifice, he found himself in prison on death row for a bogus charge. Jesus was out healing the sick, raising the dead, and freeing the prisoners, but He hadn't yet made any attempt to help release John from prison. Maybe John's mind betrayed him. Did he wonder if Jesus was threatened by John's own ministry and the loyalty of his followers? Did he think Jesus wanted him out of the picture?

Who knows what went through his mind in those last days, but we do see a glimpse of what he was struggling with in the seventh chapter of Luke. We're told he had heard the rumors of the miracles Jesus performed. You'd think that alone would confirm to him Jesus' deity but he needed more. He needed a Savior, not a magician, and in his hour of need, Jesus didn't appear to be doing too much "saving" in John's personal life. So, he sends some of his disciples to question Jesus. In Luke 7:20 we read,

When the men came to Jesus, they said, "John the Baptist sent us to you to ask, 'Are you the one who was to come, or should we expect someone else?'"

That was a shrewd move on John's part if you ask me. We all have questions and times of doubting but

John involved the hearts of his disciples, too. He could have written the message on some parchment, sent a messenger and kept it personal between him and Jesus. Instead he voiced his concern to his disciples. Perhaps he feared he was leading them astray into believing Jesus was the Messiah. He knew that he would be executed soon and wanted to make sure they knew the truth themselves before he was gone. Regardless, it appears he felt let down and forgotten by God.

However, when I studied Jesus' answer, I was encouraged. In response to John's question, Jesus immediately performed miracles by curing people from diseases, sickness, evil spirits, and blindness. He then turned to John's disciples and instructed them to go back to John and report everything they had seen. He didn't send them away with just words, but he sent them with *proof* that would fuel John to endure until the end. He left them with no room for doubt.

As I continued to read this passage, it got even better. *After* this, Jesus didn't turn to the crowds around Him and scorn John for lacking faith or rebuke him for questioning Him as the Messiah. Instead He extolled John to the crowds and acknowledged all he had done to serve God. He even went so far as to call John the greatest man to be born of woman. We may not know what caused John to doubt but the important part is

Jesus knew that John was scared and fear can cause us to act out of character. Jesus didn't hold John's doubts and questioning against him. He didn't put a notch under John's name in the Book of Life as a reminder to have God deduct a blessing in Heaven from him. Rather, He addressed his doubts and praised John in spite of it all.

Later, in the midst of His own fear, Jesus Himself would question God the Father. He made a bold petition to God in the garden before His crucifixion,

Father, if you will, please don't make me suffer by drinking from this cup. But do what you want, and not what I want.
Luke 22:42 (CEV)

Even on the cross He cries loud enough for others to hear, "My God, my God, why have you deserted me?" (Matthew 27:46 CEV). Was He feeling pain of abandonment similar to John the Baptist? Who knows — but Jesus experienced a strong human emotion that day and in the midst of it He cried out and questioned God. His doing so, along with His response to John the Baptist's doubts, led me to believe that perhaps Jesus opened that line of communication between God and us; that He welcomes the questions of those seeking real answers.

This told me that Jesus knows it's scary down here on Earth. He knows that when life doesn't go my way I have uncertainties and anxieties. If my faith is being tested, I'm tempted to run away and take an easier route. But God is God and He doesn't have an inferiority complex. He can handle my questions. He knows if I'm truly seeking to know Him and find the truth. Jesus loved John and had no problem with John doubting His deity. To me, it felt as if this was God telling me to go ahead, "Bring it on!" My interrogation was something that He could handle. It wouldn't separate us and it could even draw me closer to God.

chapter 4

God can be hard to find

How can I be sure that God is with me daily?

When I was young I had my first love, or so I thought. It was your stereotypical first "love" relationship. We spent hours on the phone. I doodled his name during class and dreamt of spending the rest of our lives together. One day, though, things began to change. The phone calls started to come less often and on the weekends he needed more time to hang out with his friends. It was only a matter of time before I learned he was calling someone else and that *someone* was becoming more important to him.

My heart was broken and I thought I'd never love again. This event left a scar on my heart. I felt betrayed. Someone I thought was committed to me actually had been lying, sneaking around, and cheating on me. After this it was hard for me to completely trust the men I dated for there was always a part of me that wondered if I was once again being played for a fool.

This fear filtered into my relationship with God. The Bible told me that God is always with me, but how could I be certain when I couldn't see Him and know for sure? Would He be there when I really needed Him or would I be left looking ridiculous?

❈ ❈ ❈

I've always been fascinated with the marathon. I couldn't imagine someone running 26.2 miles and to me, this seemed like an unreachable goal that was only for people with long, skinny legs. My legs are short and stubby so I figured it wasn't for me. Before we married, Mark had run a couple of marathons but the stories from his races did nothing to convince or entice me to attempt the distance myself. In one race he puked at mile two, was hit by a car at mile twenty-one, and by mile twenty-three he was so fatigued that he stole oranges right out of the hand of a female spectator, literally. I assume she was holding them for a loved one of her own. If by chance you are the marathoner who had to suffer through the last three miles of the Atlanta Thanksgiving Day marathon with severe hypoglycemia because my husband stole your oranges, I apologize and you have my permission to hound him with obnoxious e-mails.

After our two-year term in Chile expired, we transferred to Munich, Germany for our next assignment. Six months later, our daughter Anastasia was born and we fell in love with our new home. Every October, Munich hosts a marathon that runs throughout the city into their large park, Englischer Garten, and then ends in the Olympic stadium that hosted the 1972 Olympics. We had been in the country for a little over a year and decided it would be fun to head to the stadium and watch the end of the race.

We took the train to the stadium and found seats where we could see the runners enter the stadium and cross the finish line. It was a dramatic setting as the first few runners entered the stadium one at a time and ran a lap around the track to the finish while Olympic-themed music blared. A little time passed, and the crowd of runners thickened. All of sudden the announcer shouted and the crowd cheered louder jumping to their feet. "The first female. Here comes our first female runner!" The music was cranked and we all went wild. A small woman wearing a running cap entered the stadium and waved as she ran by us. I got emotional. Anastasia, who was nine months at the time, was in my arms and I lifted her up as we cheered. Not quite sure why I did this. It's kind of embarrassing now that I think of it but part of me was celebrating being a woman. For years women had been told they were too weak to cover the distance and now here was a woman, finishing a marathon strong and not too far behind the male winner. It was inspiring.

We continued watching as the more "normal" people finished the race. Some runners cheered and some cried as they crossed the finish line. Awed, I kept thinking, "Wow, all these people just ran a marathon." I could have stayed there all day watching, but our kids were young so boredom quickly consumed their good moods. As we were leaving, another loud cheer broke out in the crowd. I turned to see a female runner entering the stadium and hanging on to her left hand was a little boy with his short legs running hard alongside her. Someone had handed him over to her in order for him to join her in her lap around the stadium. She was a normal-looking woman and mother of a young child . . . just like me.

I was moved as I watched them cross the finish line together. It occurred to me then that I had been sitting on the sideline, watching others achieve a goal I secretly held and I knew at that moment that I could do it; I had to do it. It was time for me to enter the race and give it a try.

❦ ❦ ❦

I went home and ordered a variety of marathon books off the Internet. I always had been a novice runner and had never run more than six miles. I began researching training plans to figure out which one would work best for my fitness level and life phase. I spent the next year slowly building my mileage and then eighteen weeks out from the race, official marathon training began. It had its challenging moments with sick kids, work conflicts, and other time constraints. But each week I accomplished another goal by running a distance I had never run before.

The morning of the race I woke up nauseated, but not from illness. I suffered an attack of nerves and I asked myself, "Why the heck am I doing this by choice?" I had an overwhelming fear that I wasn't going to be able to finish the distance. My family and friends knew that I was running that day and I didn't want to embarrass myself. The only thing helping me was the fact that Mark would be racing with me. When I told him the year before that I wanted to run the marathon, he registered, too, and offered to run with me and act as my caddy. He would wear a fuel belt that would hold my water and sport gels that would give me energy to finish the race.

Race day weather was perfect. It was overcast and cool as we lined up at the starting line. My only goals for that day were to finish and have a good time doing it. The gun went off and we began. We ran through Munich and its many beautiful sectors. At mile six, I felt great. "I might be able to finish this race with no problem."

In my marathon books, I had read about something called "The Wall." It's when your muscles are depleted of fuel and your legs feel like lead, making it hard to move. It usually attacks between miles fifteen and twenty but can often be avoided if you refuel properly and keep a proper pace for your fitness level. Mark was working hard to do both for me. He would pass me my sports drink when I needed it and kept an eye on the clock to make sure we kept the correct pace.

However, as we approached mile seventeen, my legs were weary and I feared "The Wall" was approaching. We turned a corner and I saw we were about to enter Englisher Garten, the huge city park. We'd be in it for three to four miles and I hoped the change of terrain and scenery would help me forget about my legs.

At the entrance of the garden was a man, standing alone, holding a huge sign that read, "Where there is pain, there is life." A shot of adrenaline passed through me. These words spoke so much truth. I was feeling pain but it was a reminder that I was alive, accomplishing a goal that I had desired for many years. Only a few years prior I had torn my ACL in a skiing accident and after the surgery I could barely walk or bend my knee. But now, I was running a marathon.

The race progressed and the fatigue in my legs returned. We were out of the park and back on the city streets. At mile twenty-three we came upon a huge crowd and a DJ playing music. The crowd had pushed onto the street and formed a narrow passageway for the runners to run through, much like the fans do in the mountains for the cyclists in the Tour de France. The DJ was pumping up the crowd, "Here come our heroes! Cheer for them! Cheer for them!" As we passed through the human tunnel, men, women, and children cheered us on as if we were the professional cyclists in the Tour. They shouted words of encouragement and patted us on our backs. There was a new pep in my step. It was the push I needed to get me to the end.

We were getting close and had about a mile and a half to go when it hit me, "I'm going to make it. We're almost done. I'm going to do it!" The words flooded out of my mouth but emotions came with them. I tried to control them but my fatigued state couldn't stop them. My sobs stole oxygen that my body desperately needed and I was beginning to hyperventilate. Mark spoke to me and calmed me down, "Focus. Focus on the run. We'll celebrate in a few minutes." His words redirected my energy and I was able to pull it back together and concentrate on the final mile. I rehearsed in my head the Bible verse mantra, "I can do all things through Christ who strengthens me." The words took my mind off my emotions and onto the goal ahead of us.

We continued on and within minutes I heard the Olympic music and could see the entrance to the stadium up ahead of us. We ran another few hundred yards, turned right, then entered the tunnel leading us into the stadium. We headed toward the track and began our lap around as the crowds in the stadium cheered us on. Mark shouted over the noise, "You did it, baby. You finished it. You're about to become a marathoner!" We came out of the last turn of the track, onto the straight, and crossed the finish line together. A volunteer walked up, congratulated me, and put a medal around my neck. I couldn't believe it. I just ran a marathon!

❂ ❂ ❂

Later that afternoon, I reclined on the couch with my tired feet propped up. I relived the day in my mind. The man with the sign and the "Tour de France" cheering section were two big pick-me-ups that got me through some low points in the race. Positive written and verbal words did wonders to push me through the pain.

Days later, I watched our kids play. We had given them our medals as a gift for patiently enduring the weekends filled with us taking turns doing our long runs. They still wore them proudly around their necks and were acting out the final stretches of their own personal marathon. Anastasia had picked up my water belt and was pretending to be drinking water. As I watched her, the realization struck me: it was Mark's constant presence with me during the race that was my biggest source of strength. His talks kept my mind off my discomforts. He encouraged me when I faltered. He stopped at each water station and refilled my water bottles so I could keep running. He even wore my water belt so I wouldn't have to bother with the extra weight. The only reason Mark ran that day was to help me. He would stay with me, for better or for worse, no matter how it turned out. It was a complete act of love and sacrifice and it broke my heart that it took me days to realize that I had taken for granted all that Mark gave me.

I thought about this more and wondered, "Do I do the same with God?" The cheers of man distract me from God's constant presence because the applause of man makes the "race" louder and more fun. God may use their spoken and written words to get me through rough patches in life but it's He who carries my yoke and burdens so I'll have the energy to get to the finish line. He's the one who guides me. He's the one who protects me and provides all my needs. Could it be that He's *so* present that I don't always see Him, the same way I neglect to see the beauty of the foothills that I see daily?

Mark's help was very visual that day; I was just too preoccupied with myself to see it. How many times has God's companionship been visible to me but I chose to look at myself instead?

❁ ❁ ❁

Priscilla Shirer is one of my favorite authors. In her Bible study, *Discerning the Voice of God,* she points out that we're often frustrated by God's "delay" to answer our prayers or make his presence in our lives known. She uses the analogy of God as an air traffic controller and us as the pilot. Now the air traffic controller is not only responsible for us, he's also looking at other planes in the air and those still on the ground. We, the pilot, may be radioing in, ready to land, but the controller needs to make sure all other parties are in their place. If another aircraft is in our path when we land, the results can be catastrophic.

This was a great visual for me. It reminded me to take my eyes off myself and remember that just because God is at times silent or not easily seen doesn't mean He's not at work. He's lining up things, getting them ready. He's sending me encouraging words through His other children. Even though I don't see His hand,

He's the one holding up the sign. He's the one patting me on the back and cheering me on. He's the one who's carrying my water belt. He is the one lining things up, getting them ready so He can give me the call and let me know that it's safe to land and move on with my journey.

He's always with me in the daily activities of my life. I just needed to retrain my eyes to see Him interacting with me through the words and actions of others and in the beauty of His creation. It didn't happen overnight. It took conscious effort before the mind and heart followed and seeing God in the small things became second nature. However, I quickly found if I quit looking for Him, it was hard for me to hear Him, especially when hard times hit.

chapter 5

God is a bully

Does God dread?

I enjoyed my time of reconnecting with God. It was like a courtship. I spent more time reading the Bible and was able to see more of His personality that I had overlooked in the past. At the same time, there were parts of the Bible that turned me off, especially when I read the Old Testament. God the Father in the Old Testament seemed harsh, legalistic, and emotionally distant. Was He a bully?

In Bible college I sat through numerous theology classes that explained away this thought I had about God. He was protecting Israel from its pagan neighbors. He used the law to show us our need for a Savior and was paving a way that would reveal Jesus in the right time. This all made sense and I believe it to be true but there is an emotional side to me, one that

God Himself gave me, that needed to reconcile with this issue before I could go further in my courtship with God.

* * *

In late November 2004, we vacationed for a few weeks in Thailand visiting Mark's brother, Jeff, and his wife, Tara, who worked in Bangkok at the time. We spent a couple of weeks in the city and a week at the beach. The kids were almost two and three years old at the time so we were up early every morning. We would have breakfast in an open-air restaurant that was a hundred yards from the ocean — heaven on Earth. The scenery was incredible and the people were kind and hospitable.

In December we headed back home to Munich, Germany, and were quickly consumed with the holiday season. The morning after Christmas, I checked my computer and read that a tsunami had hit Phuket, Thailand, and other countries in Southeast Asia. As time passed, news of the story and devastation grew.

Thousands of Germans were in Phuket that Christmas. In the following weeks, German television covered stories of families returning home but without their complete family. Parents shared the horror of eating breakfast with their children that morning and then watching as the wave washed them away, never to be seen again. One couple hung on to a tree for hours as debris in the water crashed into their bodies, not sure when the nightmare would end.

A journalist interviewed an Australian mother who had held onto a tree and both of her small children. The waves were too strong and she didn't have the strength to hold both of them. In order for any of them to survive, she had to let go of one. She had to choose. She let go of the oldest, thinking he'd have the best chance to survive on his own. She screamed as she watched the water carry him away, and then realized he'd probably never make it. Later she and her husband searched frantically for him and miraculously found him in a makeshift hospital, alive. You think it would be a happy ending but there was no joy in their eyes as I watched them in an interview. How do you recover after making such a decision and then living with the emotional scars?

It was horrible. I often imagine myself in other people's predicaments. I visualized our hotel. I could see the wave rushing into our open restaurant. We, too, would have been at breakfast. Many mornings I was there alone with the kids. What would I have done as the waters swept? Could I grab them both? Would I have to choose one of them to grab? I couldn't answer. I didn't want to have to answer that question and I begged God never to cause me to make that decision.

Then I got angry. "Why? Why did it happen at Christmas — one of the busiest travel times?! Why did it occur at such a vulnerable hour, when young families were eating breakfast and childless couples were asleep, oblivious to the danger that was about to invade their hotel rooms?" You'd think God would want them to have a chance at survival.

Did God care or is He just a big bully? What did He feel watching the horror of the day's events unfold? Did He close His eyes, not wanting to see His loved ones suffer or was He emotionally distant? What did He feel the day before that Christmas day? If He's all-knowing and aware of what was about to take place, did He dread knowing that hundreds of thousands of people would lose their lives tragically that day?

I wondered, "Does God ever dread?"

On September 10, 2001, did He have a sense of dread knowing the next day planes would fly into the World Trade Center, thousands would die and families would be torn apart forever? Children would continue to wait by their front door for months, wondering when mommy or daddy would return home. Women would give birth months later, alone, without the loving kiss of their husband. Newborn babies would forever be without their fathers. Did God dread that day?

Did He dread the morning of December 14, 2012, as little girls in bright tights and boys in boots kissed their parents goodbye and walked into their elementary school, when He knew that in a matter of minutes some would be facing a horrific death and others would live the rest of their lives with the nightmares of a gunman murdering their teachers and friends. Did God dread that morning?

What goes through God's mind as He anticipates the onset of such disasters?

Natural disasters have always been a sore spot for me. So often many of the victims seem to be the poorest and least among us. Why does God allow tornadoes to hit trailer parks and those most in need of some stability in their lives? Why do earthquakes hit developing countries where their structures are the weakest? Why did Hurricane Katrina head directly into the Gulf Coast and devastate the most vulnerable people in the city?

All my life I had excused these questions away with Sunday school answers that put a bandage on the wound, but deep down an infection festered that was slowly spreading throughout my heart and it was time to ask God, "Are you a loving God or are you a bully?"

Does God dread? This question intrigued me. I wondered when there is tragedy on Earth, does He close his eyes or turn His back, not wanting to watch

His children suffer? Is He tempted to intervene and stop it? I had never thought about God before in these human terms. Does He have *all* the same emotions as we do? Not sure of what to think, I passed it off as a non-essential. Initially, it wasn't anything I really *needed* to know. Instead I was mainly curious. But the question wouldn't leave me and I was oddly excited when I thought about it — almost as if God wanted me to pursue it.

A few weeks later, I was attending a conference with some missionaries. Many had theological training; a couple of them were former pastors, some with doctorates. It was like being in a room with walking Bible commentaries. One evening after our meetings, a handful of us were hanging out together. I've always enjoyed sitting in these groups and listening to the conversations because eventually the current event or hot controversial topic would be brought up and debating would begin.

This particular evening, there was no discussion going on so I decided to ask their thoughts on whether or not God was emotionally detached from our disasters. It was not long after the 2004 tsunami so I asked, "Do you think God dreaded the day before the tsunami hit Thailand?" Everyone was silent for a few moments as they thought it over. Then, Joe (not his real name), one of the former pastors spoke up, "I don't think it makes much difference to God. Most of those who died weren't His children and were never going to believe in Him anyway. It probably doesn't matter to Him if they all die in one day or if they die throughout the next sixty years. Either way they are going to hell."

I felt sucker punched. I wasn't expecting an answer this harsh and it hurt. Prior to this I had sensed a compassionate side of God but if this was how God really felt, I now questioned if I wanted to have anything to do with God. Was I that far off to think that God shared in our emotions? In Joe's defense, he had answered off the top of his head and didn't have much time to process my question fully. However, it showed me a view many have of God: much like Santa Claus. If you act right, you're on the "good" list; if not — sorry, but there is no next time. I've always been a late bloomer in life and seldom got anything right the first time around — so if this was true, it was not good news for someone like me.

How could I love with all my heart, soul, mind, and strength a God who was so carefree about natural disasters and the death of the lost? I wasn't sure if I agreed with Joe. I'm not a theologian but something in me wanted to believe there was more compassion in God's heart, not only for His children, but also for those who still didn't know Him. Was this my own personal desire, how *I* wanted God to be, or was it truth? I became obsessed with this topic.

A friend suggested that I read Philip Yancey's book *Disappointment with God*. I devoured the book, for he addressed many of the same issues with which I wrestled.

There have been times when I've been a victim of heartache as a result of living in an imperfect world, so I was curious to read Yancey's take on how God reacts to the suffering of His children. Throughout the Old Testament, God had watched the Israelites suffer because of the evil of others. Their land was invaded and they were led into captivity. Their temple, the place where God dwelled with His children, was destroyed by the Babylonians. In his book, Yancey highlights Isaiah 63:9 to illustrate God's response and the pain He feels:

> *In all their distress he too was distressed, and the angel of his presence saved them. In his love and mercy he redeemed them; he lifted them up and carried them all the days of old. (pp. 94-5)*

We live in a fallen world and bad things are going to happen to us as a result of sin, but this verse gave me hope. God feels the pain of His children and we are not alone in the midst of our trials. He longingly waits until the day He can redeem us.

But I know myself; I'm hardheaded and therefore I can be a hard one to love. Much like the Israelites in the Old Testament, a lot of my suffering has been self-inflicted. What does God feel when His children suffer because of their own sin? Ahab is known as one of the most wicked kings of Israel; however, he was given numerous second chances. In Ezekiel 33:11, we see that God often intervenes in our lives in an attempt to save us from our own demise:

As surely as I live, declares the Sovereign Lord, I TAKE NO PLEASURE IN THE DEATH OF THE WICKED, but rather that they turn from their ways and live. Turn! Turn from your evil ways! Why will you die, O house of Israel? (Emphasis mine)

These verses reminded me of the paternal side of God. Like a loving father, He is merciful and doesn't rush to punish His children but instead waits in hope of us turning back to Him. But what about those who have yet to be adopted into His family? Some curse Him, others deny Him but there are also those who do these things based on their culture or how they were raised. Moab was a constant enemy of Israel. The Moabites refused to aid the Israelites on their way out of Egypt. They hired Balaam to curse them and often induced them to join in their evil sacrifices, luring them away from God.

You would think God would be eager to wipe them off the face of the Earth but in Jeremiah 48:31 we read:

Therefore, I wail over Moab, for all Moab I cry out,
I moan for the men of Kir Hareseth.

God not only mourned, He *wailed.* It wasn't a whimper but a heartfelt cry, the kind that takes over your whole being. And, it wasn't just for a handful of people who were seeking Him. The verse tells us He wailed for *all* of Moab, the good, the bad, and the ugly. He didn't sing out His own praises with, "Who's the Man?! Uh huh, that's what you get," type of attitude. No — instead His heart broke over what He had to do in order to keep Israel pure.

These verses were therapeutic, for they helped me to see that the God of the Old Testament is a God of love. It gave me the freedom to see that I serve a God who does not treat us like action figures that He playfully uses to destroy each other. He's not one eager to send earthquakes, tornadoes and other disasters to watch us flee, much like a child who kicks an ant pile in order to watch the ants scatter in fear.

No. He suffers when His children suffer. He takes no pleasure in the penalty given to His children when we rebel. He mourns for the death of His enemies and rejoices when we repent and return to Him. He is a

just and compassionate God and what more could we
ask for?

❀ ❀ ❀

Years later, our family spent part of the summer
in Thailand once again as Mark did research for his
dissertation. The first few weeks were filled with
excitement but as the weeks went by, the kids and
I were plagued with homesickness. One night I was
awakened when Anastasia crawled into bed with us.
She cuddled into me and cried, "Mommy, I miss my
family and friends back home." I wrapped my arms
around her, "I know, honey, I miss them, too," and we
cried together. After a while, she kissed my cheek, "I
love you, Mommy!" and then headed back to her bed.

The next morning she was back to her old self and
eager to play with the little girl she had befriended
down the street. Nothing in her situation had changed.
Her words didn't change; her circumstances and her
tears didn't erase the pain. However, I believe the time
she spent in my arms and my crying with her, sharing
in her pain, gave her the comfort, stability, and peace
to help her embrace her situation.

Unfortunately, painful events will continue to
invade our broken world. Orphans will wake up
without parents, widows will end the day alone,
doctors will still give heartbreaking news, and natural

disasters will continue to strike. But we have a God who is distressed when we suffer and wails with us over destruction. I may not know the *why* behind such things but, like Anastasia, it gives me great comfort and peace knowing that I do not cry alone but instead I have a loving God who'll wrap His arms around me as we cry together.

And nothing feels as good as being in the arms of a loving Father.

chapter 6

is God safe?

Can I trust God when tragedy hits home?

Our family has two black labs named Louie and Gracie. We bought Louie from a backyard breeder when he was a puppy and rescued Gracie from the Humane Society. They are wonderful dogs but have very different personalities. Gracie is submissive and timid. Louie, well, Louie is not. He loves everyone and thinks each person was put on Earth to play with him. When he sees a kid, he thinks he's amongst peers, develops tunnel vision, and loses his ability to hear our commands — then darts off to play with the unsuspecting target.

I took him to puppy potty training school, during which he walked to the middle of the class circle, hunched his back, and proceeded to poop in front of everyone. To finish it off, at the end of class, he peed on the instructor's foot as she was giving me further instructions. It was not a proud moment for me.

He and I later attended puppy kindergarten together in order for me (and him) to learn some basic commands. Instead of learning, he spent each class trying to wrestle with whichever puppy classmate was sitting next to him while I nervously laughed and apologized to the other owner. After a while, people quit making eye contact with me when we walked into class as if hoping we didn't see them and would sit elsewhere. All that was missing was a pair of "dunce" hats for both of us to wear.

In desperation, I watched hours of *The Dog Whisperer* and began implementing all that I had learned in hopes of bringing calmness back into our lives. In time Louie's behavior improved and we were able to entrust him with some new freedoms. He learned it was wrong to teethe on the siding on the house (that was a painful period) or the kid's stuffed animals (this was a tearful period). He began nudging his nose on the blinds to alert us when he needed to go outside to do his "business" instead of picking his favorite spot by my side of the bed (thank you, Jesus). He even improved on our daily walks to pick up Anastasia from kindergarten.

On our walks I befriended another mother from Anastasia's kindergarten class who had a puppy named Tanner that was near the same age as Louie. One day she brought him for kindergarten pickup in order for him to meet Louie. The dogs immediately hit it off and began wrestling. They were still on leash and it knotted as they flopped around. Our kids were running around playing and the rest of the kids had gone home so we figured it was safe to take them off leash. They remained in a pile of wrestling dog fur so we believed we had accomplished a new milestone: the dogs will stay nearby when off leash.

Anastasia's kindergarten was a half-day program but some kids stayed full day and ate their lunch after the half-day kids went home. The dogs were doing well and our kids were playing next to us so my friend and I took our attention off the dogs and were engrossed in conversation. About this time the after-school kids went marching by us about fifty feet away. It was right before Thanksgiving and they were carrying trays filled with turkey, gravy, potatoes, and rolls. I'm not sure if it was the kids or the smell of the food that caught Louie's and Tanner's attention but they stopped playing, looked toward the kids, and darted off at full speed.

Oh, no! Oh, no!!

"LOUIE!! Stop! Louie, no! Oh, no, LOUIE!" It was too late. He was in tunnel-vision mode and didn't hear my voice, or maybe he did and just chose to ignore it.

The line of kindergartners saw two fifty-pound pups rushing them and began to scream. Some put their trays down and ran; others stood frozen in fear. Their caretaker, who had a strong Russian accent, screamed, "Poot yoor trayz up! Poot yoor trayz up!!" as she tried to grab the fleeing kids and salvage as much of their lunches as possible.

My friend and I darted after the dogs. Tanner had already confiscated a roll. Louie was jumping up on some poor kid when he saw me coming after him. He dashed away playfully, perhaps thinking I was engaging him in a game of tag. Compounding the problem was my coping mechanism to sometimes laugh in tense situations. The teacher didn't seem to appreciate my reaction and she glared at me as she shuttled the kids and what was left of their lunches into the trailer that housed the after-school classes.

It's funny now but as we walked home I feared being called into the principal's office the next day and then banned from the school grounds. Needless to say I had lost trust in Louie being off leash until he had further training.

❋ ❋ ❋

Trust is not given freely; it has to be earned over time. I wanted to trust God fully with all aspects of my life but how could I trust an invisible God when I couldn't hear Him speaking to me?

My greatest fear is the idea of losing one of our children or my husband. I was beginning to trust God on the international circuit, but what about when it hit home? What if my child were to get sick or my husband were to be involved in a terrible wreck?

Six months after Anastasia was born, I had a vivid nightmare: Someone was trying to kill my baby. The two of us were together and I was trying to hide her from her attacker. Right before he found us, I woke up. It was very realistic and I can still see some of the images in my mind today. It was similar to the type of dreams where you wake up believing your dream to be true but then realize it was just a dream and are filled with relief. The only difference was that I didn't feel any relief. It still felt real, almost as if it were a warning. I woke Mark, crying and telling him the details. He tried to comfort me, reminding me these dreams are normal after a pregnancy but I insisted this was different. So we prayed together for her safety.

The dreams continued. After each one Mark and I would pray together and go back to sleep. A few months later Mark woke me up. He was really shaken for he had experienced a similar dream involving Anastasia. Our prayers became more fervent as we prayed for our daughter's safety.

A few months later I received a disturbing e-mail from my sister-in-law, Tara, who was still living overseas in Thailand. She apologized for sending her message in an e-mail but it was the middle of the night in Germany and she felt an urgency to let me know as soon as possible. She too had a graphic dream about Anastasia's death and felt God urging us to pray for her safety. Later that day we spoke on the phone and I could hear the emotion in her voice. Prior to this, I had never been one to think much about dreams but this was getting freaky. I shared with her Mark's and my dreams and she pledged to join Mark and me in praying.

A few months passed and, thankfully, the dreams stopped. But, as is human nature, so did my prayers for her safety; that all changed one cold day when we were returning home from a walk. We had a big snow that year and everything was beginning to melt. We lived in a row house that shared a walkway with two other families. Normally I would keep Anastasia in her stroller until we got to our door. She had a tendency to stomp on our neighbor's flowers on her way to our house.

This time she wanted to get out of her stroller and walk to the door. She wiggled and threw a tantrum. For some reason, this time I decided to give in instead of fighting her. Seconds after she left the stroller, a huge icicle that had been hanging on our building broke off and landed in the stroller right where she had been sitting. Mark and I stood paralyzed witnessing what could have been. I don't know if the icicle would have killed her but it would have certainly caused serious injury. This near accident was enough to wake us up and continue praying for safety. Maybe God was trying to tell us something.

❄ ❄ ❄

It was the worse day of my life.

We were still living in Germany. The row house we lived in was narrow but was three stories high with winding marble stairs. Anastasia had recently turned two years old; she was my shadow and followed me continually up and down the stairs, mimicking my every move. She was stable in her walking but she wasn't ready for what I called "German step aerobics" and had already had a few tumbles that were horrifying to watch.

I worked busily that morning getting ready for an overnight guest. The drain to the guest shower that was on the top floor was partially clogged so I used a spoon to pour Drano crystals directly into the pipes. Anastasia was with me, chattering in her own world as I worked. I gathered the cleaning supplies and together we walked down to the next floor. To save time and to keep Anastasia from walking up another flight of steps, I gathered some laundry to wash before moving to the ground floor.

I had the spoon I used with the Drano in my hand. In the process, some water had gotten on the spoon and some of the crystals were stuck to it. I put the spoon on a shelf so I could get the laundry. A voice in my head told me that it wasn't safe but I blew it off. The apartment was so narrow, I figured I could get the laundry and be back in seconds.

It only took seconds until I heard an explosive scream. I turned to see Anastasia holding the spoon, stomping her feet and crying in great pain. Thankfully we were in the bathroom so I quickly picked her up and began rinsing her mouth over and over. It didn't matter; the poison had already begun its damage and her lips and the inside her mouth were beginning to swell.

Mark was at the U.S. embassy that day, working on our visas. He had called me earlier to let me know that he would not be allowed to take his phone inside with him so he'd be out of contact for the next hour. Moments prior our team leader had called me so I knew he was at home. He was an American but had been raised in Austria as a missionary kid. His German was perfect and he understood the German medical system better than any of us. So I called him and he rushed to our house and took us to the hospital.

In the car Anastasia immediately fell asleep. Her mouth was severely swollen and her face looked deformed. Thankfully, though, it had not reached her throat so it didn't affect her breathing. However, I wasn't sure if it was safe for her to sleep. I attempted to wake her up but she would barely open her eyes and then they rolled into the back of her head as she fell back asleep. My mind was playing tricks on me. Was she dying? What was happening inside of her?

It was time for me to make the dreaded call to Mark. He was still away from his phone but I needed to fill him in. His phone went straight to voicemail so I left him a message with a brief summary of what happened, let him know that a friend was picking up Noah from kindergarten, and told him to meet us at the hospital.

At the emergency room, the staff moved us ahead of everyone and sent us to another ward. As we walked up I saw the sign in German that stood for Pediatric Intensive Care Unit. "Oh, God! No! Please no! Intensive care is where adults go, not children!" There was a hopeful part of my brain that wanted to believe it was just a blister and would be gone in the morning.

A doctor observed her and had an IV put in her arm with antibiotics to help prevent infection. She had second-degree burns in her mouth and he felt she was safe but wanted to perform an endoscopy in order to make sure there were no internal burns. Anastasia had eaten breakfast so they would need to wait a couple of hours before performing the procedure. Since she would be staying overnight, they went ahead and moved us to her room. My team leader had a flight later that day so he needed to leave but he had been so gracious in sacrificing his morning to help me. He was a true godsend.

A while later, another doctor entered the room to explain the process of the endoscopy and let me know they would be taking her soon. Mark arrived while we were talking. The concern on his face turned to fear when he saw Anastasia's face and I broke down for the first time, "It's my fault! It's all my fault!" The doctor left us alone. I had not acted responsibly. It had happened on my watch and the worst part was that something in my head had told me not to leave the spoon on the shelf. Was it my own conscience or had I missed the voice of God?

There was a tap on the door and a handful of nurses were there with a bed, ready to wheel her to the operating room. Anastasia, who had been sleeping in my lap, was nervous when we woke her so they allowed me to carry her. Once we were there, a team of masked men and women began hooking up different tubes to her IV. They allowed me to keep holding her until she was under the anesthesia but warned me that once it reached her system to be careful because she would go out quickly. She looked lifeless as she went under. The nurses took her from me and asked me to leave but I felt as if I were leaving my baby in her hour of need.

Mark and I waited and prayed.

After an hour a nurse hurried into the waiting room to get me. Anastasia was in recovery but was having a reaction to the anesthesia and the tubes attached to her body scared her and she was flailing and screaming. The endoscopy revealed she had minor burns on her esophagus and they feared her cries would further damage her burns.

I followed the nurses and I ran to Anastasia's side. I tried to calm her down but she was focused on the cords connected to her and continued to scream and cry. She had a hoarse, croupy-sounding cough. I asked the nurses if I could try holding her. They worked to loosen and remove unnecessary cords to help me reach her.

I scooped her up and spoke into her ear, "Anastasia, it's Mommy. It's okay, baby. I'm here with you." When I spoke into her ear she recognized my voice. She knew her mommy was with her and immediately calmed and nuzzled into my neck.

Miraculously, the swelling was mostly gone the next day and there was only very minor permanent damage. Compared to what could have been, we were very blessed.

But the story didn't end there. My careless actions could have had serious consequences on my daughter's future. I felt I needed to wrestle with God over this. Why had He not stopped me? Why would He allow an innocent child to suffer because of the actions of her mother?

I had heard a voice in my head. It was clearly telling me that it wasn't safe to leave the spoon in that spot. During my time of battling this out with God, He reminded me of this voice. In Isaiah 30:21 it reads, "Whether you turn to the right or to the left you will hear a voice saying, 'This is the road! Now, follow it'" (CEV). I believe now it was God's voice, warning me. However, like my dog Louie, I had tunnel vision and was tuned in to my "to do" list instead of hearing His still, small voice. Anastasia was much the same when she awoke from the anesthesia. It wasn't until I spoke into her ear that she could hear my voice over her own noise, but it wasn't just her hearing my voice, it was her *recognizing* my voice. It was then she was able to calm and relax in her mother's arms.

God is a spirit and therefore invisible to our human eyes but He works to make Himself known to us. God was reaching out to me and trying to warn me of the danger. My problem that day wasn't in not hearing His voice, but instead it was in not recognizing His voice — and that takes time. It may require me to go the extra mile, to ask the embarrassing question, or to enter into an uncomfortable situation. But following His voice will lead me down the correct road and there is no safer place for my family or me than in the center of God's will.

chapter 7

Jesus is boring

*If He were walking on the Earth today, would I drop
everything to go follow Him?*

While I was in school, my parents were actively
involved in the lives of my siblings and me. My mom
was always a room mother and my friends loved her.
She sewed the costumes for the school plays as my
father helped build the scenery. During homecoming
week, my father was always one of the loyal fathers
who helped construct the base of our parade float and
then moved aside for us to decorate it. I was proud
to be their daughter and loved being associated with
them.

Unfortunately, this hasn't always been the case
with God. And, to be honest, depending on the crowd,
there have been times I've even been embarrassed to
be associated with Jesus. Many would say that being a

follower of God isn't all that cool. If the name of your God is *Jesus*, it becomes all the more uncool. It wasn't because of anything He did — there was plenty to be proud of: turning water into wine is pretty unique and it surely trumps my dad changing the flat tire on my bicycle. It was more who He was, as in His personality. From my childhood, I remember the pictures of Him lining the walls of our Sunday school classroom. Jesus always looked so solemn and almost depressed or bored. In the films we watched, He always spoke in monotone and only half-smiled, unless of course He was snidely talking to the Pharisees or turning over tables in the temple. He was never portrayed with a full-bellied laugh or joking around with the disciples. He wasn't someone that I'd ever invite to go on vacation with us. Of course this is only man's interpretation of Christ through art but perhaps this subliminally influenced me into thinking that Jesus was a bit . . . boring.

I believed Him to be God and my Savior. I knew He was hard-core and I was extremely grateful for the sacrifice He made for mankind. However, deep down, I wondered: if He were walking on the Earth today, would I drop everything to go follow Him? If I were in a coffee shop, working on my laptop, and He came in and said, "Leave it and follow me," would I walk away from my computer in order to be with Him? Would

I cash in my kid's college fund and our retirement and give it to His entourage? Would I remove the roof shingles from my neighbor's house and lower my best friend into their living room in order for Jesus to heal her? I'm not sure what I would do but He would have to have more than a few good tricks to convince me. There would need to be something special about Him that would cause me to leave everything behind. It felt as if I was missing something in regard to Jesus. I wanted to know, what was it about Jesus that motivated the masses to follow Him? What did they see that I was missing? What caused me, at times, to hide my association with Him? I wanted to be proud to be in His family, not ashamed.

I'm not proud of this, but in the past I was rarely drawn to read the Gospels unless it was required for a study. I preferred to focus more on some of the other books in the New Testament, like James, where the teachings were more applicable to *my* life. Yes, I was an egocentric Bible student. However, I knew I needed to step out of this habit. Jesus is the visual we have of God, the second head in the Trinity. I knew if I seriously wanted to love *all* of God, I needed to rediscover what first attracted me to Him when I became a Christian.

I had heard and read the stories about Jesus numerous times. Perhaps that was part of my problem.

I knew them so well that as I began to read them as a refresher, I'd often skim over the text. Could it be that maybe I was missing some important details? I decided to reread these stories but this time with a fresh set of eyes. In the past, I always focused on Jesus. This time I was going to look more at the people in the crowds and see if I could figure out what drew them to Jesus. You can tell a lot about a person by the people who hang around him and you can learn a lot about a leader by the people who follow him. I hoped as I looked more closely at the crowds, I would see more of Jesus.

Throughout the Gospels, there was often a large group of people following Jesus. But I had a hunch that not all of them were truly seeking God. Jesus was probably walking entertainment in a time without television or the Internet. I'm sure many of them were hoping to see a freak show or to keep up on the latest gossip, "Did you see Jesus heal Mary, the one with curly hair, yesterday?"

"The tall one or the short one?"

"The tall one. I always knew she had a demon in her. She's as mean as a stepped-on snake." Some stuff is more interesting to experience in person.

Of course, many were there hoping to be healed from the ailments and deformities plaguing their lives and to be the next recipient of His many blessings. But, as I studied more of the details of these stories, I realized my assumptions about the masses were not necessarily correct. Maybe they were more than fair-weather followers and Jesus provided something else they really needed.

In Matthew 14:13, Jesus has just learned of the beheading of His cousin, John the Baptist. He retreated and boarded a small boat to cross the lake in order to be alone. The crowds learned of this and followed Him on foot in search of His new destination. This is not the most sensitive move on the crowd's part but they didn't want to be separated from Jesus. When He stepped off His boat, He sees them, has compassion for them and begins healing the sick among them.

As the evening drew near, His disciples nudged Him to wrap up the healing session. "This place is like a desert, and it is already late. Let the crowds leave, so they can go to the villages and buy some food" (CEV). I'm guessing it is safe to say that there were no fast-food restaurants nearby. They were aware of the hour and their hunger pains reminded them that it had been a while since they had eaten. I get their thinking: there have been times during church when my stomach has made itself known to the masses sitting around me. At that moment, my focus is no longer on the words of our pastor, but instead on the food I would eat once he was finished. My only thought is how I can get out of there quickly to avoid the after-church lunch crowd. Not so with these people. Even though it was getting late and they'd have to journey by foot in the dark, they did not want to leave Jesus, and it didn't sound like Jesus was in a hurry to shoo them off. He said, "They don't have to leave. Why don't you give them something to eat?" (CEV). The disciples handed over five loaves of bread and two small fish they had gathered. Jesus multiplied them and they were able to feed more than five thousand people.

The next chapter recounts a similar story of Jesus in Galilee. Another large crowd gathered around Him, bringing to Him people who were sick — and He healed *all* of them. He then called to His disciples and said, "I have compassion for these people; they have already been with me three days and have nothing to eat. I do not want to send them away hungry, or they may collapse on the way." *Collapse on the way?* They were really hungry and way beyond my foggy-headed hunger.

Something about Jesus kept these crowds with Him. They were away from home for days and had run out of food. Was there something in Jesus that caused them to want more? I'm sure they were initially there to be healed but what kept them there for three days? Why didn't most of them head home after they had been healed? I looked at the description of the people.

Matthew 15:30 says the crowd was made up of the paralyzed, the blind, the lame, people who couldn't speak, and the loved ones who brought them. These were the social outcasts of that time period. They weren't able to work and had to beg for a living. Their day was spent watching people look through them, as if they didn't exist. They were the bullied. Never touched. Invisible.

There were others in the crowd too — the same verse tells us that these people were *brought* to Jesus. Maybe it was parents who had watched their child shunned by others because of a birth defect, or a brother who had grown up speaking for his mute sibling, or a husband who carried in his blind wife, hoping Jesus would restore her sight. They, too, had spent their lives being rejected because they loved or lived with someone who was "different."

But the verse tells us that Jesus healed *all* of them. They weren't there still waiting to be healed. Why didn't they leave after He had healed them? There must have been something else that Jesus gave them. Was there something different about the way He looked at them or touched them that made them want to stay? His compassion and love were beyond anything they had ever experienced before and it overrode their need for food. Jesus saw them. He touched them. Jesus didn't look through them. He looked into them and listened to them. He loved them.

I could relate to this need. Growing up I was the shy child who was often overlooked when I was away from home. I was well behaved so I didn't require disciplinary attention, but I was not attractive or funny so there was nothing to cause others to see me. It's a horrible feeling being the unseen person on the sidelines. Mrs. Farmer, my fourth grade teacher, was the first to see any potential in me. She placed my desk next to hers and gave me the extra attention I needed to develop the confidence I lacked. I loved being around her. She made me feel special and *believe* there was something special about me.

When I looked at Jesus through the crowd's eyes, I realized, Jesus sees each of us — and especially those who feel invisible.

As I continued reading, I discovered the crowds weren't made up of outcasts only. In Mark 5:21, I read about Jairus, a synagogue ruler. He was a leader with power and influence and, unlike many populating the previously mentioned crowds, he had something to lose — his position and reputation. He risked looking foolish. His daughter was dying so he went looking for Jesus, the man who, once again, was surrounded by a large horde of people. He may have been tempted to wait until Jesus was alone but his desperate situation called for drastic measures.

Jairus joined the crowd but he didn't try to blend in; instead he made a scene. He fell at Jesus' feet and begged Jesus to save his daughter. That was a gutsy move especially when you consider that Jairus was the head of the synagogue and that Jesus had a growing reputation of being hard on spiritual leaders. Still, Jairus, a man of power and influence, humbled himself before Jesus and possibly humiliated himself before his friends and co-workers. Jairus must have seen power and truth in Jesus and was willing to throw away his status in order to receive Jesus' help. Even those with worldly status saw something different in Jesus.

While I was in school, my college hosted an annual Mission's Week on campus. They'd cancel classes for the week and bring in missionaries and representatives from various mission agencies to speak to us about their ministries and the many things God was doing around the world. Throughout the day we attended breakout sessions that lasted about an hour each and at night we'd have a main speaker in the chapel.

It was during the late 90s and a hip man in his early 40s from Colorado spoke of a new way his church was ministering to Generation X. They didn't meet in a church setting but instead in their home. Their teaching style involved more discussion than lecture. It was a new way of reaching a younger generation. As he spoke I felt energy surging through my soul.

This was it! This could be the ministry that God was calling me to do.

After his session I waited in line to speak with him. I was a junior that year and was looking to fulfill my internship requirement that summer. My hope was that he'd be thrilled to have free help for the summer. Plus, I had taken time off school for a few years to go to Russia, so I was an older student with experience. I figured it would be an easy "yes" for him.

It was my turn and I began to share my thrill of hearing his testimony and how I'd love to learn more about his ministry. He was excited to hear my praise and interacted with me until I asked if he had any openings for summer internships. He looked beyond me, put his finger next to his mouth, thinking and then turned back to me and asked, "Are you engaged to be married?"

Thinking he was concerned that I'd be the type of girl to leave my internship early because I missed my fiancé, I was proud to answer, "No."

"Do you have a boyfriend or think you'll be getting married soon?"

Weird question but I figured I was still on the right path. "No. I'm single."

"Have you ever thought about being a missionary?"

"Uh, yes. That is my major." I still wasn't following his thought process.

"Good. However, unless you are willing to do children's ministry, there are very few churches who would ever think about hiring you. I know it sounds harsh but I don't think there is any way my church would ever consider bringing you on in this ministry."

I didn't know how to respond and I could feel the burning in my eyes. To his right were two male classmates. One looked blown away as much as me. I thanked him for his time and hurried back to my dorm trying my best not to cry in public. My stomach churned and my heart ached. Never before had I felt like a second-class citizen because of my gender. Why would I feel such a strong pull to go into ministry if God saw me unworthy of a ministry that I was drawn to?

The next day "Mr. Colorado" found me in the cafeteria and apologized for his words. He claimed he didn't agree with the rules about women working in his church but he didn't want to lead me astray knowing that there would never be a job for me there. I appreciated his concern and continued to focus my studies on international ministry but another scar was left on my already floundering self-esteem.

God had made me a woman and I didn't want to believe that He considered me a second-class citizen based upon my gender. Furthermore I didn't want to believe that He thought less of people because of the color of their skin or nationality. I needed to know how Jesus saw me as a woman. I needed to understand what He thought about others of a different race.

❖ ❖ ❖

I continued studying the crowds and noticed there were a lot of women hanging around Jesus — I was pretty confident it wasn't because He was a ladies' man. The prophesy in Isaiah 53 tells us He wasn't handsome and that there was nothing about His appearance that would attract us to Him. So I guess that meant He wasn't a looker. As I began scouring the stories involving these women I saw why they were so drawn to Him: He gave them value and worth.

In John 4, Jesus approached the Samaritan woman at the well. A woman, who was of a different race. He encouraged her not to find her worth in sex but in the living water He offered her. His disciples were surprised to find Him speaking to a Samaritan but Jesus knew what He was doing; many Samaritans became followers of Jesus that day. God had chosen her to help Jesus reach them, people that *God* wanted in His family.

In Luke 7, Jesus was a guest in the home of a Pharisee, a church leader, when a sinful woman came in and bathed His feet with perfume and washed His feet with her tears and hair. Jesus defended her to the men. Her act of love was beautiful and He praised her to the group of leaders.

It was a different world for women during the days that Jesus walked on Earth so His actions were magnified. He not only cared for women, He gave them worth and even used them personally in His ministry! God had chosen the woman at the well. Jesus knew she would passionately share His message to other Samaritans. Jesus saw her, a woman, worthy of the calling.

Jesus valued women. He saw their heart; He saw their pain and He gave them worth. This touched me. God may have given me a different role, but He did not see me as second class. He valued me.

Jesus cried over the death of Lazarus but celebrated at the wedding of family friends. He didn't hang out with those obsessed with laws but instead was a friend of sinners. There was something magnetic about his personality that drew people to such dramatic acts. If anything, Jesus was not a dud. He was the life of the party, the comforter of the soul, the healer to the sick, and the giver of life. And if you ask me, He is not a God to be ashamed of, He is a God I'd run to.

And there is nothing boring about that.

chapter 8

where is the Holy Spirit?

Does the Holy Spirit help ME?

Growing up, I received teaching on God the Father and God the Son but not much on God the Holy Spirit. He was the mysterious part of God that I equated to my conscience — the internal God police that would poke and convict me if I was breaking one of God's rules.

It's not easy to love a rule enforcer, especially when you have a bad habit of pushing boundaries. Proverbs 21:19 says it's better to live in the desert than with a nagging wife. At that time I had the faulty belief that the Holy Spirit was an inner nagging wife that pointed out my faults and reminded me of my failures.

But I also heard miraculous stories of how the Holy Spirit worked in the lives of people — a missionary who escaped danger after a stranger knocked on his door, a check arriving in the mail the day before a family was to be evicted, a lonely single woman opening the Bible and reading a verse that gave her special encouragement. The list goes on and on. I loved hearing these stories and wanted them to be true because they meant that God's Spirit still worked personally in the lives of His people. And yet, if they were true, it also meant something else — the Holy Spirit *wasn't* active in my life.

I did have my own stories of stressful situations resolving at the last minute or finding Bible verses that encouraged me in times of need, but they were sporadic. I didn't want a God who randomly showed up like the absent father who visits his kids a few times of year, lavishes them with gifts only to take off again. No, I wanted and *needed* a God who would meet me in times of crisis but who also would walk with me daily. Could I find this in the Holy Spirit? Was He already doing this even though I hadn't seen it?

Jesus told His disciples in John 14 that He would not leave them as orphans but would ask His Father to send a Helper or Advocate, the Holy Spirit, who would help lead them into all truth. This sounds wonderful in theory, but based on my personal experience, it felt as if this Helper played favorites and I was not on the popular list.

Perhaps my definition of the Holy Spirit limited my ability to see Him. Maybe I was hiding behind a safe filter that was preventing me from experiencing Him in my life, both in the big and small ways.

How can you love a God who seems absent? At times He felt negligent when I needed His touch the most. I now saw the compassionate side of God and I was becoming more and more proud to be associated with Jesus, but had I ever been touched by the Holy Spirit?

I was speaking about this to a friend of mine and she told me to try to remember a time when I felt God's presence in my life. Pray about a moment when His presence seemed stronger than any other and then dissect it and look for ways that God was active. Trusting that God would reveal something to me, I started praying.

❋ ❋ ❋

In 1995, I was twenty-eight years old, single, and on a team with seven other people working in orphanages and schools in a small town in southern Russia. The Iron Curtain had fallen, but Western influence and all the good and bad that it brings had just begun trickling down from Moscow into our town. Food was no longer scarce but times were still tough. We had to take a forty-five-minute train ride to a larger town in order to find pasteurized milk, and even then we weren't guaranteed of finding it. This wasn't a time of abundance.

One time, my teammate, Susan, and I went to visit a friend in the hospital. Our neighbor, who was also a friend of this patient, went with us. Susan and I were horrified as we walked into the tiny hospital in our town. It was as if we'd entered a door that took us back in time. There wasn't much equipment around and what was there was so archaic, I couldn't believe that it still worked.

After visiting hours we said our goodbyes, merged with a group of three other women who were also leaving, and headed toward the hospital's main door. It was chained shut. In our search for an open door, a man who was bleeding from his abdominal region cornered us. He held an IV cord, which apparently he had yanked from his body, and grunted slurred words at us. "What he's saying?" I asked our Russian friend. She didn't seem to hear me so I asked her again. "What's wrong, what's he trying to tell us?" Again, she didn't answer me.

Nervousness filled the faces of the women around us as they scurried around the ground floor, looking for an open door. Uneasy, we stayed close to them until we finally found an opened side door and rushed out into the darkness toward the parking lot. Once inside our car our friend told us, "The man was crazy. He said he'd kill us unless we helped him get out of the hospital."

I remember thinking: *"Oh, thank you, Lord, that I never have to be a patient here!"*

❀ ❀ ❀

The pain jolted me awake. I had gone to bed early trying to sleep off an aching stomach. Through the night it had migrated down the middle of my stomach and was now in my lower right side. It was a sharp and burning pain. My skin was on fire but my body shivered and my teeth chattered like a hypothermic skier. I had tried to stick it out until morning, but at 3:00 a.m., my inner voice said, "Get up now! You have appendicitis and need help!"

From my roommate Beth's room, I retrieved *Where There Is No Doctor*, a book to help people living in areas with limited health care. I flipped through the pages and turned to appendicitis and read *my* symptoms. Beth leaned in my doorway, "What's up? Are you okay?"

"I'm not sure. I think I have appendicitis."

She went into help mode and called Oxana, our neighbor downstairs. Oxana told Beth to send me to her apartment and she'd call the ambulance to get me to the hospital.

The hospital! NO, Lord! Please, not that hospital!!

I was paralyzed. I couldn't go there. To me, it was a symbol of pain, discomfort, and fear. I suddenly wanted my parents like the three-year-old with a bad dream calling out to her mom and dad in the middle of the night. I walked out our front door, into the stairwell and began to cry. My tears turned to panic as I descended the four stories from our apartment. *Lord, I can't do this. I can't. Please don't make me go there!* My body froze. I couldn't move forward and at that point was willing to choose any other option. I stood there, clinging to the railing when a verse from Psalms popped into my head. It was from a passage we had studied in our team Bible study earlier that week.

> *Wait for the Lord; be strong and take heart*
> *and wait for the Lord.*
> *Psalms 27:14 (NIV)*

It had come from nowhere but was so clear. I was to be strong and wait for God. It was enough to slap me out of my panic attack and bring peace to me in the midst of my fear. I could wait. I would be strong. I would be okay, right?

Oxana met me at her door, ushered me to her couch, and went to wait for the ambulance, leaving me with her thirteen-year-old daughter. Her daughter began caressing my hand and told me her mom's own appendicitis story, "When Mom had appendicitis, they went to numb her but the needle broke. They didn't have another needle so they had to strap her down and perform the operation without drugs. She went into shock!"

I don't know what it feels like to be in shock but I was pretty sure this story was about to put me into it! She must have seen the terror in my eyes because she added, "But don't worry! Our hospitals are much better now!" *Oh, Lord, I think that I've waited long enough. I'm not strong, and it's probably best that you go ahead and take me now.* I wasn't afraid of dying but I did fear the process of "getting dead" and I was even more terrified of what it would be like in that particular hospital.

The ambulance arrived and the doctor confirmed that I needed to be admitted to the hospital. There was no stretcher, so I walked hunchbacked by pain to the ambulance and was directed to a chair in the army-looking van with a red cross painted on it. There was no bed, only springy seats lining the interior of the van that bounced at every bump and pothole. And I felt every one.

The ambulance pulled up to the hospital and we were instructed to walk in through a side door. The pain in my side intensified and I could barely walk but there was no wheel chair. An orderly took my vitals and led us up a couple of flights of stairs. Each step sent a burning pain throughout my right side.

The orderly took me to a room that had a single bed in it and told me to lie there. Beth needed to call our team leader, Rick, who had been working with our supervisors and insurance, trying to figure out what to do. Our insurance required that in emergency situations like this, I was to be medevaced to Finland but we were experiencing a hiccup. We lived in a region not too far from Chechnya, during the time of the Chechen rebellion and Russian airstrikes. We were considered a war zone and it would take time to get air clearance for a plane to land in the airport that was forty-five minutes away. There were only two phones in the hospital, so a nurse took Beth and Oxana to the office for them to work with Rick to decide our next step.

I rolled onto my left side in the fetal position. It was the only way I found some relief from the increasing pain. I faced the wall that was splattered with what appeared to be some sort of bodily fluid. Anxious thoughts of infection rushed through me. Our town was in the middle of a drought and we only received water for about an hour every third day. The Russians did great with making do with their challenges but, with limited water, was the staff able to keep the hospital sterile enough to prevent spreading germs and disease?

My pain was increasing and my circumstances were declining, "Oh, Lord, I DON'T want to die without my parents. I really *need* my mom right now!"

Wait for the Lord; be strong and take heart and wait for the Lord.

I continued to meditate on this verse each time I began to lose control and each time I was filled with peace.

❊ ❊ ❊

Beth and Oxana remained by the phone as Oxana helped translate back and forth with the Russian doctors. Rick was working hard to get me evacuated but the Russian doctors were telling him I didn't have much time before my situation became serious. Oxana was doing a great job translating but had taught herself English and was not versed in medical terminology. This made Rick's ability to make a decision all the more difficult because we couldn't get a clear diagnosis.

I remained in my room alone, chanting my verse over and over when I heard a knock on the door. Stuck in the fetal position, I turned my head to see Vera, a fellow team member. She was the mother of four grown children. She and Ken were the only married couple on our team and often filled the parental roles for a team made up of singles. Just seeing her brought me warmth and relief.

She sat next to me and rubbed my back. "I don't know if there is much I can do to help you but when I heard about your situation, I felt God telling me to come sit with you. All I know is that if this happened to one of my daughters and I couldn't be with her, I'd want another mother to comfort her for me."

Had God heard my cry for my mother? Did *He* really send Vera to me as my surrogate mother? All I know is that it felt good having my "mom" with me — surrogate or not.

❋ ❋ ❋

My pain continued to worsen and the doctors told us that I needed to have surgery soon and offered to perform it for me; they even went as far as calling in their chief of surgery. I told my teammates that I wanted to have the surgery in Russia. My pain told me that I was running out of time and I was desperate to bring an end to it. However, my supervisors were still hesitant; they didn't want doctors performing surgery on me until they were sure of the diagnosis.

So we waited on the Lord some more.

I continued to face my wall and chant my verse when Beth entered the room, smiled big at me, and said, "You are not going to believe this but two American doctors just walked into the hospital. They are here on a humanitarian trip. They have a Russian doctor with them who speaks perfect English. He said you have appendicitis. It's the simplest operation to perform as long as they get to it before it bursts. The American doctors can't perform the surgery for insurance reasons but they agreed to be in the room and observe the operation. They even have clean syringes and antibiotics and will give some to you!"

God had given me peace through the Bible verse but now I had joy. I had not imagined it. God gave me that verse and was aware of my situation and it appeared that these doctors were part of what He wanted me to wait for.

We all saw this as God giving us the "okay" and it was time to roll. The doctors went to scrub and prepare for surgery. It was time for me to head up to the operating room, but there was no moving bed or wheelchair and no hospital gown. A nurse motioned for me to put on my shoes and follow her.

Hunched over, I followed her down a winding hall and then up another flight of stairs. Oxana asked if she could go with me and help translate and they agreed but she would have to scrub in once we got there.

We walked into the operating room and I saw a team of men wearing masks and what looked like tall chef hats. I chuckled as many jokes flashed through my head. Oxana interrupted my comedic thoughts and said, "Laurichka, they want you to take off your clothes and climb up on the operating table." (Oh, which was metal, by the way . . . and cold.)

I looked back to the group of chef-looking doctors who were still watching me and then back to Oxana. "Uh, right here?! Do they have a gown I could use?"

One of the nurses sensed the reason for my hesitation and brought me a sheet. Since I was unable to stand up straight, Oxana helped me undress and wrapped me in the sheet as the rest of the room stood at attention and watched. A nurse escorted me to the table and motioned for me to climb up on the table. The pain prevented me from being able to lift my leg and in my struggle to climb up I lost the sheet. "& #@%!" I wasn't proud but I'm pretty sure the Russians were able to translate this word because they all came to my help at this moment.

Once I was on the table, the nurses and men wearing chef hats and masks sprang into action and began strapping my arms and legs to the table. *Why are they strapping me down?* Panic coursed through me once more.

Wait on the Lord; be strong and take heart and wait on the Lord.

Their faces were masked but their eyes smiled and were filled with compassion, as if sensing my nervousness. Someone took hold of my hand, caressed it and then spoke to me in a warm, Midwestern accent, "Looks like you got yourself in a bit of a mess."

I looked toward the voice and discovered it belonged to one of the American doctors, an anesthesiologist. He began explaining what the medical team was doing and what would happen after the surgery. I would remain on the operating table post-surgery until I woke up. The breathing tube would remain in my throat; once they saw me awake, they'd turn off the airflow and if I began to gag, it showed them my natural reflexes had kicked back in. Not to panic, this was the norm.

He continued to hold my hand, making small talk. Having him there with me brought a strong sense of security, peace, and warmth. I felt safe and protected. Soon they administered the anesthesia and I slowly began to drift off to sleep.

I had felt the Lord's presence during my appendectomy. There were so many ways the Holy Spirit manifested Himself to me.

He was my Guide and Helper. When I was alone in my apartment in the middle of the night and in such pain, God's Spirit directed me not to stall, to immediately wake up Beth, and to call Oxana who then guided me and acted as translator through the Russian medical system. He instructed me through the surgery and recovery via the American anesthesiologist.

There were numerous times throughout the night when anxiety and worry attacked and each time the Holy Spirit encouraged me with Psalms 27:14 or Psalms 91. These verses cleared the noise in my head and allowed me to rest in the promises of God.

The Holy Spirit also comforted my aching heart. Even though I was twenty-eight years old, I wanted my parents. I longed for my mom to care for me the way she did when I was sick as a child. I never prayed or asked God for my mom's presence but *HE* knew that desire of my heart. When He sent me Vera, it was a personal touch and showed me that God knows what we need, even before we ask for it (Matthew 6:8).

He never left my side. When the American anesthesiologist held my hand before my surgery, the peace that flooded my soul was indescribable. It felt as if the Father Himself stood there beside me saying, "Don't worry, my dear. I'm here with you. It's going to be okay." And He held my hand until I fell asleep.

❀ ❀ ❀

I love reliving this story. The Holy Spirit felt so present but I wondered why I didn't sense him like this on a daily basis.

A while back I went for an early morning run. Mark
and I were in the beginning phases of our business
and the financial insecurity of it was weighing on me.
We had sent out numerous invoices that remained
unpaid and things were getting tight. It was at the
peak of the financial housing crisis and I feared this
was a sign of how our business would go and we could
end up losing everything. So as I ran, I prayed. At the
end of my run I turned onto a trail behind our house
and began to walk the rest of the way home. I felt so
alone and God was quiet. Where was His Spirit of
encouragement? I really needed Him at that moment.

To my left were the Boise foothills, gorgeously
decorated with the sunrise. I felt a nudge to praise
God but I didn't really want to. I was irked with Him
because I needed security in that moment but heard
nothing from Him. But then I felt another poke, "Who
do you think I am?"

As I looked at the foothills an awkward praise came
out, "You are gorgeous. You are the most creative
being of all. Thank you that I can see such beauty each
day." Each word came out more easily and my critical
"Where are you God?" heart soon became an open
heart, one willing to hear and see Him. I continued
praying, "Lord I don't know what to do. I don't know
what to ask for. If you would, please shine your light
on Mark and me and show us what to do. Please shine
your light on our path!"

The trail I walked on turned to the right and in the distance I could see our house. The sun was rising and at that moment it was shining through a break in the trees. The rays of the sun were settling just on our house, illuminating it like a spotlight as the other houses surrounding it remained shaded. Was God literally shining the sun on our house? I know it may sound odd being excited about the sun shining on your house but I believe it was God's Spirit showing me He had heard my prayers. He had answered my prayer *literally* and it let me know He saw what we were going through. It gave me peace and reminded me of His presence in our stressful circumstances.

I called Mark when I returned home and told him about the sunrise. He could have laughed it off as coincidence but he, too, saw it as God putting His arm around me, encouraging me to hang in there. Nothing changed in our finances that week and worry continued to attack but, each time, I tried to replace my fears with the reminder of God's shining light. It gave me confidence to believe that God was still with us and would help us get through whatever came our way.

The following week I opened our home mailbox and found a check that had mistakenly been sent to our home address instead of the office. I called Mark to tell him the good news, "Thank you, Jesus!" The next day, as I waited in the carpool line at the kid's school, Mark called me, "God's shining on us! We just got another check!" We had breathing room and each day that week we either received a check or a purchase order. "God is shining on us," became our new mantra for each time we experienced a blessing and grew to be our own personal reminder that God *sees* us and is *with* us in the extreme and daily activities of our lives.

There are still those moments when I feel alone and overlooked by God but that is usually when I've gone into my egocentric and control-freak mode, wanting a genie instead of a God. However, if I can break free and turn my eyes back to God, it's not long before I see the Holy Spirit sending me reminders, whether it be another person holding my hand when I'm scared or God shining His sun upon my life. He's always with me and lets me see Him. It just takes me opening my eyes.

chapter 9

i'm too busy to love

Why do I feel so overwhelmed?

One day I was sharing with Joanne, an older and much wiser friend of mine, some of the struggles I was going through with God. She looked me in the eye and sternly said, "Laurie, there will come a time in your spiritual walk where you won't struggle as much with the big sins. At this point you must be careful, because if the Devil can't get you bad, *he'll get you busy.*" Her comment threw me — what did my schedule have to do with my love for God?

We finished our meal together but when I went home her words clung to me. Part of me was a little offended. Did she question what I was doing with my life and use of time? I mean, everything I was doing was good stuff and, in fact, "God stuff." But then I wondered, what is *God's* stuff? Was I doing what He

had planned for me to do in my daily life or was I acting out of guilt and playing a role and living certain standards that weren't necessarily of God?

Busyness is a plague in our culture and I'm often embarrassed if I don't have a long list to share if someone asks me what I did that day. I have a tendency to be like Martha, running around volunteering and completing my "to do" list, but this mostly comes from guilt. I really want to give in to my Mary side and spend the day meditating on God's word but part of me fears if I do, I'd like it too much and could easily spend my days in my sweatpants, praying, looking out the window at the trees with one of our pets nestled on my lap as the laundry piles up and the food molds in the fridge. The only thing preventing that from happening (besides the fact that Mark and the kids would snap me out of it) is the thought of someone knocking on the door and catching me being still. Oh, the embarrassment! Psalms 46:10 tells us to "Be still, and know that I am God," but in James 2:20, I read that faith is useless unless it's backed by deeds. How am I to balance the two?

Years ago our son, Noah, was diagnosed with celiac disease and could no longer eat foods containing gluten: basically, anything with wheat, barley, or rye. For a bread-eating, pasta-loving person like me this meant relearning how to cook in order for him to thrive. The gluten had prevented his body from absorbing the nutrients in his food, so he wasn't growing and his blood work revealed that he was malnourished.

Upon hearing his diagnosis, I immediately went into mama mode. I began researching and trying new recipes that would keep food fun and tasty but, frankly, was having little success. Broccoli quiche was one of Noah's favorite meals so I thought I'd try to recreate the recipe using a rice flour crust recipe that I had found online. However, that night I couldn't get the crust to stick together and had to keep tweaking the recipe. Everyone was getting hungry and I was tempted to ditch the whole thing but I had no other gluten-free alternative for dinner and we had yet to find a pizza restaurant that delivered gluten-free pizza. So I kept working at it.

Ninety minutes later the oven timer went off and I was excited about my accomplishment. I reached into the oven and pulled out a perfect-looking quiche, unaware that our seventy-five-pound Labrador, Louie (it's always Louie!), was behind me. As I backed away from the oven with the hot quiche in my hands, I stepped on his paw, lost my balance, and dropped it onto the floor. Mark claims I spewed out some "wordy durds" in the process. I don't recall this but perhaps the cortisol flooding through me momentarily blacked out my memory.

I couldn't believe it. All that hard work was now a heap of hot mess on my kitchen floor. Louie understood my wordy durd and took it to be his signal to make an emergency exit. I then yelled, ahem . . . I mean, *called* everyone into the kitchen. Mark looked at the splattered quiche and said, "What happened?'

"Louie was behind me when I took it out of the oven!" Everyone's head nodded in understanding — everyone knows that it's always Louie! "Everyone get a fork," I instructed as I grabbed my utensil, sat on the kitchen floor next to "dinner" and started eating.

Anastasia quickly joined me, "Okay, this looks good!" (Yes, she is her mother's daughter).

Mark and Noah stood behind us, holding their forks, watching. "Really?"

"Yes! This is dinner. I spent too much time on it for it to go to waste." (My parents would be so proud of me at this moment.)

Mark kneeled by me, preparing to join us when he noticed a dog hair on the floor next to the quiche, "Nope, can't do it. I'm going to Alberstons to buy fried chicken." *Okay that sounds better!* We scooped up the top layer of the quiche that had not touched the floor and salvaged enough to make Noah a plate. Not a move to win me the Mother-of-the-Year award but we were desperate. Luckily, he was hungry enough and excited to have his favorite meal again so he didn't let the memory of the dog hair haunt him.

We laugh when we retell this story now, but when I think of this time, I remember it differently. I felt overwhelmed. We were all at our limits. The first time I went to the grocery store after Noah was diagnosed, I cried — literally. I didn't know what I could safely buy without making him sick. My cooking time had doubled, our food budget tripled, and the variety in our meals narrowed. It was hard — at times very hard — and I overreacted to the quiche episode because I was on the break of burnout.

It wasn't until we discovered some friends who were also gluten free that I felt a sense of release. They came to my aid and taught me that this new lifestyle was very doable and could be affordable but it would require me to make some adjustments. I had to revamp my shopping list and cut out certain items in order to stay within our budget. To plan for meals and ensure Noah's food needs were covered, I would need more time to prepare for vacations and sporting events. I had to keep cupcakes in the freezer at all times so we could take our own to birthday parties. In order to make his life feel more normal, and for me not to go crazy in the process, I had to reprioritize my schedule.

Yes, the new lifestyle was a struggle *but* it wasn't a burden because I love Noah. I love him with all my heart and when you love someone you do what it takes.

❊ ❊ ❊

A while back, my kids and I went to the smaller, pricier grocery store by our house. We only needed a few things, and like always, I was in a hurry. The kids were restless and complained as I darted down each aisle in a race against the clock. I looked like a human mini-van weaving around other customers when another shopper forced me to slow down. My cart faced the backside of a little ol' grandma who had parked her cart in the middle of the lane, her body blocking the remainder of the aisle as she looked from one shelf to another. She turned to see us waiting. We smiled at each other and she greeted Noah and Anastasia and then went back to her shopping.

She seemed oblivious that we were unable to move past her. So I did what I'd want someone else to do if it were one of my parents in that situation. I smiled and pretended to be on the wrong aisle, turned around and hurried off. However, we must have been shopping for the same items because she was everywhere I needed to be and her cart remained in the way. I was getting annoyed. Didn't she remember the stress of shopping with kids in tow? Not fun.

I finished up my shopping and shuttled the kids out to the car. As I loaded my groceries, out came the little ol' grandma and a store employee. He loaded her groceries as she chatted away. I could tell he was trying to cut her off and get back to work. I feared I was next to be chatted up. She was sweet and normally I'd love to talk with her but I needed to unload the groceries before taking Noah to his practice. So, I hurried with my groceries in hopes of pulling off before the store employee was able to get away.

Then I heard her say something that changed everything, "My husband died almost a month ago. It's so hard eating dinner by myself. I don't know how to shop and cook for just one person."

Ouch, ouch, OUCH!

I leaned my head against the side of my car, winded. She wasn't a self-absorbed shopper taking up the aisle. She was a new widow, eating alone, and learning how to survive without her husband. *I* was the self-absorbed one. I felt like a jerk. I was the jerk!

I wanted to talk with her so I stalled loading my groceries. She said good-bye to the grocery boy and turned to face me. I didn't know what to say so I commented on her fancy truck. She began telling me the story of how her husband wanted her to have a safe car in case she was ever in a wreck. "I miss him." We talked for fifteen minutes. Her kids were moving her into a condo to be close by. It comforted me knowing that she wouldn't be completely alone. She was lovely. I was late but it felt right.

I was humbled that day. God reminded me that the heart of His children is more important than the busyness of my life. My little 'ol grandma friend was a red flag, a reminder that sometimes serving and loving God is not done by doing more but by saying "no," doing less and just being present in your current circumstance.

Was it possible that my busyness was putting a glass ceiling on the growth of my love for God? There is work and effort that is involved in all love relationships but it should never feel burdensome. As 1 John 5:3 says,

> *This is love for God: to obey his commands. And his commands are not burdensome.*

Jesus said the two greatest commandments are to love God and to love our neighbor. Neither of these sounded overwhelming and I could see the natural progression. When there is true love for God, the other stuff falls into place. It may not be easy but the *love* helps you do what needs to be done. I had been doing everything in reverse. I worked hard to show my love for God, but in the process overloaded my calendar with doing good deeds so that I no longer sat still before God.

It was time to prioritize God and trust in my time alone with Him, and I believed He would then show me the where and the how.

a God i can follow

Has my love been restored?

One fall, we spent a week at the beach with our extended family. We ate most of our meals at our hotel's great outdoor restaurant with a grass roof, next to the ocean. With the exception of a couple of other families, we had the place to ourselves. On one of the first days, as we were finishing up lunch in the restaurant, Anastasia saw another little girl at a neighboring table. She slid out of her seat and made her way over to meet her new friend. Anastasia knew no fear in meeting strangers. When I noticed her new whereabouts, I scurried to the table, hoping she wasn't disturbing this family's meal.

The father, Tony, said hello and I immediately noticed his accent. He was Danish but he said they were living in Norway at the time. As we talked, he learned that we had lived in Germany doing mission work. His body language stiffened and the muscles in his face flexed, "Oh, I don't allow my kids to go to church. The world is depressing and has enough negativity in it as it is. Why would I send them to a boring church where all they hear is how bad they are and learn about a God that is not too exciting Himself?"

Uh . . . how do you respond to that? I didn't know much about the church in Norway so I didn't challenge his mini-lecture and just listened as he vented. He continued on his soapbox, berating the church until his wife, Christine, returned to the table. She looked embarrassed and immediately changed the subject. I sensed this was not the first time he had given this spiel. We talked about our vacations and learned they were overlapping; since our kids were near the same age, we agreed to look for each other at the pool or beach.

During the day, Christine often hung out at the pool with us while Tony joined the men who were kiteboarding. We shared some meals together in the restaurant and spent long hours at night talking over drinks together but the spiritual conversation never came up again.

Part of me felt guilty. Even though the relationship wasn't perfect, I had come a long way in renewing my love for God and now longed to spend time with Him.

My prayer life had been revived and I loved talking about God and was eager to learn more of Him and about Him. Why then was I now shying away from sharing Him? Was there still part of me that was ashamed of God? I didn't think so. Maybe it was the boldness and harshness of Tony's words. He was so sure of what he believed that I doubted he would even hear me if I objected to his views.

I didn't know what to do, so I did what God had taught me over this journey, and that was to be honest with Him. So I prayed, "God, I'm sorry, but I'm still embarrassed to share You with others who so adamantly oppose You. Help me know how to do it and be faithful to You."

The week continued and neither Tony nor I had addressed the topic of God or the church. I felt like a loser, already backtracking on my commitment to God. Mark and I really liked Tony and Christine — why wouldn't I want to share God with them?

On one of our last days, Christine told us that it was Tony's birthday and that she wanted to have a birthday dinner for him that night. She asked if we would join them for dinner. She was going to get a birthday cake but knew he would enjoy the night more if we all would celebrate it with him.

We had a great meal together and afterwards were sitting in groups around the table talking. Mark and

I were with Tony when he began asking about the churches we had worked with in Germany and said he was curious to hear what our organization's goals were. After I shared a little bit of its vision with him, he blurted out, "Do you really think this would work in Europe?"

My initial response was to retreat again, but there was an internal nudge to respond honestly, "Yes, I do. I believe Europe is ready to hear again the truth about God."

Exasperated, he threw his hands up and said, "Well, what is it that you believe about God?"

At first I was thrown off. Never in all my years of ministry had anyone so bluntly ask me to share my views on God. Most of the time I had to find a way to work it into a conversation but here was a guy, with strong opinions, wanting to know what I believed. God definitely had created this opportunity for me. My fear now was that I would say something that would push him farther away from God. *God, what do I say? Is what's important to me also important to him?*

I didn't know the answer to those questions, but I decided to share some of what God had been revealing to me on my own journey. Based upon what Tony had already said, I decided to focus on Jesus instead of debating Tony's view of the church. "I believe that Jesus didn't come to enforce rules but to free us from the many kinds of bondage in our world. He gave us an example of real, unconditional love. He reached out to everyone in such a way that people were drawn to Him, even though His guidance and correction were at times tough to hear. He didn't want us to have a ho-hum life but a fun and exciting life. We're not to have it all figured out but we're to keep trying to find Him and, if we ask, He will reveal Himself to us. Life is hard but that is the result of sin being in the world. God is a God of compassion who mourns when we mourn and celebrates with us. Through it all, God is with us."

Tony leaned back in his chair with his arms crossed and his face stern. I couldn't tell what he was thinking and I fought to keep eye contact as the negative voice in me screamed, "Stupid woman! You sounded like a blubbering idiot, making no sense at all. It wasn't clear; there was no four-step formula and you forgot to ask him to pray with you at the end!" Part of me wanted to flee and another wanted to hear his response.

Tony uncrossed his arms, grabbed his chair's armrest and then pointed at me saying, "Now *that* is a God I can follow!" I wanted to hug him but I knew that would probably freak him out. He continued, telling us that he wished he could find a church in Norway that believed like that.

What I shared that night with Tony was not a new undiscovered truth. It was basically the same stuff I heard growing up. The only difference is that it was delivered with a *new* heart, one that believed and genuinely felt truth in what I was sharing. I think God arranged that time with Tony not just for Tony but also for me. He revealed to me that I had broken through many of the hindrances and that my time seeking to love Him had not been in vain. I was on the road to recovery; I felt a spark of love for Him again and was encouraged to discover that I had a deeper love for Him.

Without true love for God, all my good works were frivolous efforts that would only wear me out and fill me with bitterness and resentment, but with true love for Him, I am revitalized. What once burdened me now filled me with joy and energy. Once I had a taste of what love for God could do, I didn't want to stop. I wanted to live a life that showed my love for God.

When I lived in Russia, I was in a town of 100,000 people. There was one small and very old hospital — the one where my appendectomy had taken place. There were no televisions, no food service, not much to entertain the patients, just radios that didn't work well. Needless to say, visitors were greatly treasured.

The year following my appendectomy, a teammate named Carrie and I began weekly visits with the patients in the women's ward. The women were in the hospital for weeks on end so they were eager to talk with anyone who walked through the door.

At this time, the majority of Bibles available in Russia were written in an old and difficult to understand translation. Our organization sent us copies of the New Testament that had been written in modern Russian. Carrie and I brought these Bibles with us and passed them out to the women we visited. Most of the patients were desperate for something new (and free) to read and eagerly accepted our gift.

The first week we spent introducing ourselves. We chatted a bit and tried to get to know the patients in the first room. Then, we moved to the next room of eight or ten women and did the same.

The second week, however, was spent discussing the New Testament, as most had read it between our visits. The women would load us with questions. As the weeks progressed some wanted to talk about God while others were more interested in learning about America. Either way, the women knew that we always came on Wednesday and seemed to look forward to our visits.

One week as we entered a room, a woman we had met the previous week began talking frantically.

Our interpreter, Natasha, told us the woman was concerned because a fellow patient, her friend, had been moved to another ward but she wasn't sure where. Her friend had questions for us and wanted to see us. We had the hospital's permission to work only on this particular floor but the woman was so persistent, we followed her. Up and down the floors we went, poking our heads into each room, looking for her friend, all the while avoiding hospital staff. "Maybe she went home," she told us.

There was one room we had yet to try. We knocked lightly and peeked inside. Only two beds were in this room, one man and one woman. They waved us inside. The woman spotted the Bibles we held in our hands. "What's that? What do you have?"

"It's part of the Bible, the New Testament. We are here visiting patients and giving them to those who would like one."

The woman rocked her body back and forth and started sobbing. I wasn't sure if she was upset with us or something else. She began talking quickly as Natasha listened intently to her. Natasha then relayed the story, "This is Luba. For many years she was part of the underground church. She prayed and prayed to God that He would send her someone, someone to answer her questions and bring her a Bible of her own. She said that today God had answered her prayers."

We were speechless. I felt inadequate. Before me was a woman of God who had endured hardships and persecution. She had jeopardized her life to be part of a church during Communist times, risking everything to meet with others to learn, know, and worship God. But what impressed me more was her persistence in her prayers and belief that God would one day answer them. Even fifty years later, she continued to pray and the minute it walked through the door, she recognized and celebrated God's answer.

Luba had searched for God. She didn't say a half-hearted prayer and then pout and move on when God didn't answer her immediately. Nope, she searched for Him, relentlessly, believing and waiting on Him. Part of me wonders if the celebration was all that more joyous because of the wait, because she knew then that He had heard her and had not forgotten her after all these years.

And He hasn't forgotten me. He may not answer my prayers immediately, and there may be nights and mornings where I feel my petitions are falling on deaf ears, but when the answers come, like they did for Luba, I recognize a cause for celebration and I believe that I serve a God who is real and the search for His love is worth it. He had not forgotten me, and He never will. He is working by my side the whole time. It just took me time to see it, to believe it.

We must believe that God is real and that he
rewards everyone who searches for him.
Hebrews 11:6

chapter 11

no greater love

Is loving God worth the effort?

Years ago, Mark and I were going through a rough patch in our marriage. I was in the midst of many transitions. After returning from the mission field, I had been a stay-at-home mother but our kids were older and I was in the process of re-entering the workforce. Part of me was excited but another part of me mourned my changing role. Add on top of that the physiological changes many of us go through in our forties and you could see a cocktail for a marital breakdown.

One night, after a day of trying to balance work and home life, I had an adult-sized meltdown and Mark and I had, well, let's just call it an animated "discussion." I was overwhelmed in my new role and I had been simmering for a few weeks when my whistle finally blew. Mark worked to cool me down, sharing reasons I was stressed but I felt he wasn't hearing me. Finally, I blurted out, "Mark, I'm not happy! Something is wrong and I think we need help." I hurt him, badly. I could see it in his eyes. I hated myself for saying it. I wanted to take it back but couldn't, and something told me our marriage would seriously suffer unless we got outside help.

Mark heard my plea and the next day he got the name of a marriage counselor from our pastor and set up an appointment. At our first meeting I sat nervously on the couch next to my husband as the counselor smiled at us, "Why don't we begin with you sharing why you are here."

I didn't know! I went blank and couldn't think of a single reason why I was unhappy but my eyes burned as they fought off tears. The pain was there; I just didn't know how to articulate it. The counselor then began asking us probing questions and each one took us deeper until Mark and I were able to discuss issues where we both needed help. None of it was serious but *all* of it was important because it was driving a wedge between us that would eventually sever our relationship if we didn't work together to remove it.

In time the intensity of my love for Mark was renewed and it, in fact, deepened to a whole new level. I was moved that he heard my cry for help and so quickly responded. He also showed me that he was willing to work through the crud that we had allowed to invade our marriage and, in the end, I felt a new bond in our relationship.

God heard my cry that morning back in Chile as I prepared for Bible study. I knew my love for God was in jeopardy but I didn't know what was causing it. All I knew was I no longer felt love for Him. When I shared this with Him, God, in a sense, took me through "counseling" with Him and, during the process, He revealed hindrances that depleted my love for Him and together we worked through them.

Counseling requires time, sweat, and tears and you may be wondering if it's worth enduring this with a God who is not always easy to understand. Yes — it's so worth it! As I read through the Gospels I noticed that Jesus didn't speak much about how much He loves us, rather He mainly exhorted us to love God, our neighbors, and enemies. I found this strange and somewhat disturbing but as I thought about it I realized He didn't have to tell us continually how much love He had for us. Jesus was love and when people were around Him they never doubted *His* love for them.

Why then did Jesus say over and over to "love God"?

Perhaps it was because He knew it's in our human nature to crave to *be* loved by another and if we're not careful, we neglect what is needed to truly love the other back. Regardless, it was important to Jesus, which meant that it is important to God — not because He's an egotistical God who wants us fawning over Him. No, I think it's because He knows what we receive when we are still before Him, loving Him with our time and praises. It is here where we receive His peace. It is here where we hear His voice clearly as it guides us in our daily life. It is here where we receive the supernatural energy of the Holy Spirit to accomplish what He created us to become. It is here where we see the face of God as we look at our neighbor and our enemies and then hear His voice saying, "Feed my sheep." When we do this we not only experience God's love, we become God's love to a hurting world.

Love God. His love is like no other.

epilogue

When I share my journey with people, I oftentimes hear the same questions: "Do you really think you had lost your love for God, or was it that you were not yet a Christian?" In my mind I could confidently answer that I did indeed have faith and I knew without a doubt I was a child of God. However, my journey had revealed to me that I had been negligent of my relationship with God. Like all relationships, it needed work and attention. Mark and I are married but unless I am proactive to fuel that love for him, I can remain married to him without loving him. The same can be true with my love for God.

We live in an imperfect world and the enemy is working overtime to put hindrances in our path to prevent us from deepening our love for God: doubts, fears, illness, the death of a loved one, and many more. Satan's greatest threat is when God's children are growing in their love for Him. Beth Moore once said, "When you love someone, you want to make them known." When God's children fully love Him, we will work endlessly to make Him known. As humans, it's hard not to talk about the ones we love.

My love for God is not perfect and because I am human, it probably never will be on this side of heaven — but God is faithful. When I honestly cried out to Him, He helped remove many of my obstacles and opened my eyes to some of the ways He communicates with me. Now it's easier for me to see Him. I know that He is reaching out to me when I begin to backslide or when new hardships or doubts arise. I have learned not to wallow in doubt because He has shown Himself to be present and faithful.

You may have your own hindrances deterring your love for God. I encourage you to go to God with these and be honest with Him. We don't serve a God with an inferiority complex. He wants nothing more than for each of us to open our hearts before Him. In Matthew 19:14, He told His disciples, "Let the children come to me, and don't try to stop them! People who are like these children belong to God's kingdom" (CEV). As we know, children are known for asking honest questions that come from the heart.

God delights when His children come to Him. He encourages the hard questions and appreciates that you care enough about Him to engage with Him. He knows you to your inner core and would love nothing more than for you to know Him in the same way.

As I discovered on my journey, the road to understanding wasn't always a lovely jaunt through a field of flowers, but usually a thrilling adventure that kept me breathless and engaged.

I encourage you to take your own journey, to ask your own hard questions. You will be surprised how much God will reveal if you only ask.

what next?

Many times after reading a book I've found myself asking, "What do I do now? How do I apply this to my own life?" So, I thought I'd share some highlights of things that helped me along my own journey. Most are basic but as happens a lot in life, when we return to the basics we often find new life.

Love is a personal thing and what worked for me in my relationship with God may not work for you. If it does, great! If not, perhaps these suggestions will jog your brain and give you some ideas that will aid you. Either way, I truly believe if we take the first step in recovering our love for God, He will honor it. Just remember, building my relationship didn't happen overnight. My journey was over the course of five years but each step was exciting and invigorated me to take another.

1. Go before God and wholeheartedly confess the condition of your heart.

Even if you're not sure what the issue is, tell Him. *He* knows what it is and will be faithful to guide you along the way. Ask Him to reveal the root cause. It is necessary to find the core issue, whether it be love, trust, fear, or anything else. As long as you are only treating the symptoms, that issue will continue to be a problem. Ask Him what it is that is preventing you from experiencing His love on a deeper level. He knows what you can handle and He will not give you more than you can deal with at the present. Be committed. Be prepared for anything. None of us is immune to any type of sin, circumstance, or problem in our life. If something ugly is revealed, accept it, do not deny it, and ask God to help remove it from your life. The same way that taking the wrong medication will not rid your body of a disease, refusing to address certain areas in your life will only keep you in a dead-end relationship with God. The Great Physician will give you the correct prescription.

2. Talk to someone you trust about your struggles.

Be careful who you share this with — we are to be open but not necessarily with everyone. Pray and ask God to reveal that safe person to you. A few times during my journey, God prompted me to share with either individuals or groups. Each time someone was either able to help me or I could help them by sharing what I had already learned. We are not meant to go this alone. It's much easier when we have others to help hold us up.

3. Read daily through the Bible with a new "thought" in mind.

When I say "thought" I mean whatever hindrance that God has revealed to you. As I worked through each of my struggles I'd see new points in the Bible that I had glossed over in the past. For example, I never had caught the fact that God wailed over Moab until I read the Old Testament looking for examples where I thought God was portrayed as a bully. By doing so my mind was opened up to Truth that I had missed in the past. Never stop reading the Bible. Each time you do, pray first and ask God to reveal to you the truths He wants to show you that day.

4. Read other books on the topic.

Don't just focus on your favorite authors but try someone new. Step outside your comfort zone and even read authors who may have a slightly different view from your own theologically or politically. Try reading them with an open mind. Pray and ask God to open your eyes to His Truths. Reading such books will either open your heart to something new or solidify your belief system. Highlight as you read and reread these sections later. Repetition helps us retain information and some topics require more time to process thoroughly.

5. Keep a journal as you read books.

Don't try to rush through a book, but stop often to process and give God time to show you His insight. Keep a small journal with you at all times and write down questions, thoughts, inspirations, quotes, etc., as you hear them. If you don't, you may lose them. The majority of this book came from my journals and, believe me, if I had not written it down, most of this would have been forgotten.

6. Do Bible studies throughout the year either in a group or solo.

If you are a chronic Bible study attendee, think about taking a break and doing a study on your own in order to go at your own pace. It's good to mix it up. I found sometimes I needed the accountability and insight of the group. Other times I needed the time to be with God on my own as we wrestled through a particular issue. Either way, if you are in tune with God, you'll know which one you are to do.

7. Go on walks or hikes by yourself.

Make sure you are in a safe location and have your phone with you. Do this sometimes with music and other times without. Both can help us hear God but try to do it more without the music. I found I had to be proactive in being silent, otherwise my mind would immediately think of my "to-do" list or I'd begin praying my "I want" list. I'd have to start off each walk asking God to quiet my mind and then ask Him to speak to my heart. If my mind wandered, I'd practice praising Him and that would usually redirect my mind back to Him.

8. Spend time with a generation different from your own.

Each age group has something valuable to teach us. Visit other age groups but don't focus on the externals. Don't go to the youth group and see what they are *not* wearing or how low they wear their jeans. At the same time if you go to a senior citizen's class, don't judge them by how high they wear their pants or write them off because they speak of a better day. Each generation has experienced a different life and God has given each of them unique wisdom. Don't forget, when you learn something from them, be sure to tell them. We all need encouragement and to know that we add value to the world.

9. Visit a different church or denomination and appreciate different forms of worship.

(Don't get me wrong, I'm not telling you to leave your current church or start church hopping.) I believe every congregation goes through rough or boring patches, just like marriages, and it's important to be committed and help do our part through these times. However, I do think there are times we need to be free to throw our arms up in the air as we praise God and I believe there are also times when our souls need more reverent time on our knees before God. This is something that is between you and God. He knows which form would fuel your spirit more.

10. Love and serve.

Sometimes the simple act of taking our eyes off ourselves and focusing on the needs of others is all we need to soften our hardened hearts. Jesus got up early and stayed up late in order to pray and have one-on-one time with His Father. He knew He needed this time in order to know how and where to serve. He then spent the majority of His time serving others. When our hearts are softened through serving, we're better able to feel the healing hands of God. Keep in mind that those God gives us first to serve are often those under our own roof. Jesus focused on His disciples first and then He turned to the crowds. Don't wear yourself out trying to serve those God never called you to help. Follow Jesus' model: pray first and then serve. It's in the time of prayer that God makes our call to service clear.

11. Devote periods of your life to prayer and fasting.

Jesus told His disciples there are some things that can only be conquered through fasting. It took me times of fasting alongside my prayers to work through many of my hindrances. I don't think it was a magic pill; however, it showed God my commitment and at the same time it wore me down to where I was willing to let go of some of my preconceived ideas that polluted me and kept me from hearing God. When I read the Bible with a judgmental heart, I couldn't see His truths. Fasting revealed unforgiving feelings that lurked in my heart and it silenced my overly busy mind so I could hear God's quiet voice. Be careful not to be legalistic with your fast. The goal is not the fast itself but to hear from and commune with God.

12. Be grateful.

God loves us and has blessed all of us with something. Feeling grateful is easier said than done, but even in the midst of heartache we can find reasons to thank Him. A grateful heart is a growing heart and a healing heart.

If you'd like to discuss (or debate) more on this topic with your Book Club or Bible study, download Discussion Questions at

www.russell-media.com/free-resources

Before she learned how to write, Laurie Russell
knew how to talk. . .a lot.
To book her for speaking, you can contact her at

www.russell-media.com/speakers

Purposeful Resources Transforming Society

Visit Russell Media for our latest offerings:

www.russell-media.com